LIMERICK CITY LIBRARY

:one 314668
website: www.limeri…y.ie
…lim…ty.ie

The Granary,
Michael Street,
Limerick

Blessed
MOTHER TERESA

Blessed
MOTHER TERESA

Her Journey to Your Heart

T. T. Mundakel

**SIMON &
SCHUSTER**
TownHouse

London · New York · Sydney · Tokyo · Singapore · Toronto · Dublin

First published in Great Britain and Ireland by Simon & Schuster/TownHouse, 2003
An imprint of Simon & Schuster UK Ltd and TownHouse, Dublin

Simon & Schuster UK is a Viacom Company

1 3 5 7 9 10 8 6 4 2

Simon & Schuster UK Ltd
Africa House
64–78 Kingsway
London WC2B 6AH
www.simonsays.co.uk

Simon & Schuster Australia
Sydney

TownHouse, Dublin
THCH Ltd
Trinity House
Charleston Road
Ranelagh
Dublin 6
Ireland

www.townhouse.ie

A CIP catalogue record for this book is available from the British Library

All photos courtesy of the author with the exception of
8, 9, 11, 12 © PA Photos and 14 © Mary Ellen Mark.

ISBN 1 903650 61 5

Typeset by M Rules
Printed and bound in Great Britain by
Mackays of Chatham plc

CONTENTS

PUBLISHER'S NOTE   vii

ACKNOWLEDGEMENTS   ix

INTRODUCTION   1

1   *The Path of Growth*   5

2   *The Voice of Our Lord*   20

3   *The Crosses of Obstruction*   26

4   *Caring for the Poor*   32

5   *When the Almighty Provides*   41

6   *Quenching the Thirst*   51

7   *House of Miracles*   61

8   *Opposition and Acceptance*   72

9   *The Gorgeous Path*   84

10 *Secret of Success*   91

11 *From Candidacy to Profession*   97

12 *Miraculous Experiences*   III

Contents

13 *Tents of Miracles*   122

14 *The Brothers of the Missionaries of Charity*   138

15 *In the House of New Life*   144

16 *If the Great Leaders Shower Mercy*   149

17 *Trial by Ordeal*   163

18 *Mother Teresa's Last Years*   173

19 *The Miracle that is the Missionaries of Charity*   185

20 *Mother Teresa's Last Day*   200

EPILOGUE: THE FUNERAL   206

INDEX   210

PUBLISHER'S NOTE

This book is a free translation of T. T. Mundakel's book, *Katha Parayunna Pavangalude Amma* (*Listen to Mother Teresa*). It was originally published in 1998 in Malayalam by the Asian Trading Corporation, before being translated by him into English in 2001.

ACKNOWLEDGEMENTS

It is due to the inspiration I received from the late Mother Teresa that I decided to write *Listen to Mother Teresa*, her life story. As it becomes evident from the pages of this book, I have met and spoken with Mother Teresa many times throughout her life. She would often thank God after each sentence, and so 'Thank God' appears many times in this book.

Let me also mention that I am grateful to Mary Vijayam Sahithya Samithy of Trichur for selecting *Listen to Mother Teresa* as the best life history written in 1998–99 and for presenting me with the Kakkassery Award.

Similarly, I owe a debt of gratitude to his excellency Mar Thomas Chackiath, Auxiliary Bishop of Ernakulam, Mr Babu Kadalikkat of *Deepika Daily* and Dr Thomas Kandathil MD, DM, because it was their inducement and encouragement that prompted me first to translate this book from Malayalam for the benefit of English-reading people.

With an intention to make this book as authentic as possible, I have visited several places and met many people related to Mother Teresa. Let me acknowledge with gratitude several Missionaries of Charity brothers, sisters and co-workers who were fortunate to live with and work with Mother Teresa, who have helped me in the preparation of and research for this book. They described many rare, interesting and thought-provoking incidents. Let me express my sincere thanks to every one of them without mentioning their names individually.

Let me also offer a bouquet of my deep gratitude each to Justice V. R. Krishna Iyer and Justice P. K. Shamsuddin, who were kind enough to grace this humble work with their precious appreciation.

I owe my sincere thanks, in particular, to Rev Bro Devesia MC, the former Regional Superior of South India, to Sister Sarala MC, my beloved niece, Sister Alphonsa, Sister Barbara, Sister Monica, Sister Eugien and other reverend sisters and brothers of the Missionaries of Charity. Let me also thank Rev Fr Jose Karaimadam CMI, Principal of Christ School, Bangalore, Prof V. J. Pappu MD of Deepika and all those who helped me in some way or other to publish this book.

I shall feel amply rewarded if this book induces at least one person to see and serve God who dwells in the poorest of the poor, as Mother Teresa did, making that person thus closer to the Almighty.

With respect and love to everyone,

T. T. Mundakel
April 2001

INTRODUCTION

In December 1948, with only five rupees to her name, Mother Teresa began her work in the slums of Calcutta, bringing God to the poor. 'Whoever has suffered poverty's sharp arrows alone can understand others' deep sorrows,' they say, and Mother Teresa experienced very well the misery of poverty. However, she always had great trust in the providence of God, a trust that was her inexhaustible treasure in the world. And indeed, God always provided her with whatever she needed for her work.

Mother Teresa was a simple nun, and she wanted to live a simple life. She had no desire for fame – in fact, she despised it from the bottom of her heart – but nevertheless fame came her way: she appeared on television, was interviewed, written about, filmed and was the subject of documentaries. 'I know that true holiness consists in doing God's will with a smile,' she used to say, 'and so I have always tried to smile, even when things do not turn out as I would wish. Apart from that, I don't think I have done anything worth mentioning. *Thank God.*' She always maintained that it was not she who was the object of interest in all that was written and said about her, but rather her work with the very poorest people in Calcutta. She would tell her sisters:

I am a small pencil in the hands of Our Lord. The Lord may cut or sharpen the pencil. He may write or draw whatever He wants and wherever He wants. If any writing or drawing is good, we appreciate not the pencil or the material used, but the one who used it. *All praise and glory to the Lord our God, for ever and ever.* The poor – are they not human beings? Are they not created in the image of God? Yes, of course they are. Well, then, are they not to be recognized, respected and attended to? Our loving God used me precisely to do that. *Thank God.*

Despite her wishes, however, after 1962 she started to attract the attention of the world. She needed financial assistance for her work, but she did not want fame and glory or the awards and honours that were thrust upon her. She none the less surrendered herself to the command and demand of His Grace, Dr Ferdinand Perier, Archbishop of Calcutta, and accepted the Padmashree, for distinguished service, consoling herself with the idea that the awards she received were the recognition given to the poor and the destitute; it was in their name, she reasoned, that she accepted them all – the Nobel prize, the Bharath Ratna, world citizenship and the rest.

Introduction

This book bears witness to Mother Teresa's extraordinary life. Her simple philosophy is revealed to readers and tells, often in her own words, of the inspiration and love that motivated her.

– 1 –

The Path of Growth

There is a small town named Skopje on the Adriatic shore of what is now Macedonia (then part of Yugoslavia). It is here that Agnes Bojaxhieu was born into an ordinary home of extraordinary love and grace on 26 August 1910. She had exemplary parents. They were Albanians, who had come from Prizren, a city in Kosova (then also part of Yugoslavia). Her family were townspeople, who had a long tradition of trade.

Her beloved father, Nicolas, was a leading figure in Skopje's civic life. He was well known as a member of the town council, a supporter of the arts and of the local church, a building contractor and a good businessman. He was in partnership with a rich Italian merchant and traded in a wide variety of goods. He travelled to different parts of Europe on business and spoke several languages – Albanian, Serbo-Croat, Turkish, Italian and French. Whenever he returned home, there was an atmosphere of celebration. He made all the children happy, giving them beautiful gifts, telling stories and singing songs, and took a keen interest in their education. Although he was a strict disciplinarian, Agnes always found her father kind and generous to the poor.

Her beloved mother, Dranafile, was called Nonalok by her children: *nona* means 'mother' and *lok* means 'soul'. 'Whenever I think of my mother,' Mother Teresa said, 'the word *holy* comes to mind, for by her words and deeds that is how she appeared to us.'

Her father owned a few buildings in Skopje, and the family lived in a big and comparatively comfortable house in a compound surrounded by fruit trees. Though Skopje was in a Muslim country, ruled by the Communists, Agnes was born into a Catholic family that had a deep faith and trust in God Almighty. The God of mercy gave her parents three children to be reared as part of God's family. Her sister Aga was born in 1904 and brother Lazar in 1907. The day after their young sister was born, the baby was taken to the parish church, dedicated to the Sacred Heart of Jesus, where she was baptized Agnes ('holy') Gonxha ('rosebud') Bojaxhieu. Her brother used to call her Gonxha and her family thought this name was a perfect description of her. The date she was born as a holy child of God – her baptismal day – was much more important to Agnes than her actual birth day. That's why in several records, including her passport, 27 August 1910 is entered as her birth date.

The young girl's first school was in the loving lap of her mother. From there she learned the unforgettable lesson of love – how to love God, how to love our fellow beings. She always acknowledged that she owed much to her parents, and to her mother, in particular, for her religious upbringing – learning to pray, singing in the church choir and other spiritual activities and training connected with Gospel and church. She was educated at a convent-run primary school, attached to the local church, where she received religious instruction, and later at a state school. She went readily to church services from a very early age, and this regular attendance at the parish church of the Sacred Heart gave her additional experience and inspiration. She and Aga were blessed with musical talent and they sang the solo parts in the church choir, which helped them to be closer to Jesus in the Blessed Sacrament.

Agnes was only four years old when the First World War broke out. The immeasurable misery of this time badly affected Agnes' parents, but the little girl noticed her mother's immense courage and readiness to bear anything pleasantly.

On 16 November 1916, Agnes received the Holy Spirit in confirmation, and she also received the courage to be faithful to God. The graces of the Holy Spirit would help her to face any difficulty boldly and to try to be a perfect Christian.

In 1919, God tested Agnes. Her father went to a political gathering in Belgrade, some 160 miles away. He was apparently in the best of health when he left home, but he returned in a carriage with the Italian consul, as he had suffered a haemorrhage, and emergency surgery failed to save his life. All his family members, as well as the medical profession, were convinced that he had been poisoned. He was only forty-five years old, and his sudden death was unbearable to his family, especially to his wife. They later discovered that his Italian business partner had misappropriated the assets of the business, and the family was left with nothing but the roof over their heads – and that only because the law of the country ensured it. For the first time, they experienced what it was to be without financial security. Agnes was eight. Lazar, who was only fifteen, could not be of much help to the family.

Rearing three children, giving them proper food, clothing and education, was not an easy task for Nonalok, but she put all her trust in God, worked hard, and went along the path of 'try, try, try again'. She took to sewing, embroidery and selling cloth to maintain the family. She did not allow a single day to pass without reciting the family Rosary. 'The family that prays together stays together,' she would say. If Mother Teresa repeated this to many people during her later years, the credit goes to her mother. She also taught the children that they must share whatever they had with those in need, and that there is much pleasure in giving with pain to the poor and that it is our duty to console and comfort those who are suffering.

She not only instructed her children, but also taught them by her good example. She used to wash, feed and look after File, an alcoholic woman covered with sores. Once a week she would visit an old woman who had been abandoned by her family. She cleaned her house and gave her food. When the children became aware of this, she said, 'Children, whenever you do some good to somebody, do it quietly, as if you were throwing a stone into the sea.'

One day, when the family was about to have a meal, some poor people came to their gate begging. There was hardly enough food for lunch, but Agnes' mother divided what they had into two and brought half of it to the gate and distributed it among the poor. She talked to them with kindness and love, so much so that they ate that small amount of food with great joy and satisfaction. The mother looked at her daughters, who were staring at her, and said, 'Children, they are poor people! We don't have any blood relationships with them. They are not our close friends either. Yet, they too are our brothers and sisters; they too are the children of God, Our Father. We shouldn't forget it.'

Another day, Agnes' mother brought home a basket of apples. She called the children to inspect them and they agreed that they were excellent apples. Then she placed a rotten apple in the middle of them, closed the basket and kept it in her room. Two days later she summoned the children again and asked them to examine the state of the apples. They found that all the apples in close contact with the rotten apple had also begun to rot, and had to be thrown into the bin. Then she said, 'My children, you are good, thank God. However, the moment you come in contact with bad people, you too will begin to rot like these apples. Therefore, be careful about who you mingle with.'

It was her beloved mother's sweet words and edifying example that paved the way for Agnes' vocation. During the long period of her widowhood, her mother was a constant friend to the people of Skopje who were suffering in the darkness of poverty and privation. Along with prayer and fasting, she was at the forefront of the activities of the parish church, trying to get all possible help and consolation to the diseased and destitute of the city, and she was very keen for her children also to be involved in charitable deeds. As a result, when she was just twelve years old, Agnes began to hear a voice in her inner soul that whispered: *Dedicate your entire life to Jesus Christ and try to become a holy nun.* Agnes shared this thought with her mother, but she didn't get a positive reply. Nor did her mother take it seriously, as if her daughter were lacking in physical as well as mental maturity. Perhaps she wanted to test the strength of her vocation.

From the time of her childhood, Agnes' mother had instilled in her a strong devotion to Our Holy Mother. Mary knew that she was the mother of God, and it was her deep humility and sense of charity that promptly took her to Elizabeth, her mother's sister, as soon as she heard that Elizabeth was pregnant. Agnes' mother used to tell her that she must follow the example of the visitation of the Virgin Mary in helping the poor and serving the needy with great speed. In later years, Mother Teresa would recall to her sisters the words of her mother, 'Our Lady went in haste because charity cannot wait. How nice it would be if we could all remember this!'

When Agnes was at school, Father Jambrekovic, a Croatian Jesuit and her parish priest, admitted her to the sodality, which paved the way for her cultural and spiritual uplifting. The young girl was fond of reading and it was the priest who started a parish library and supplied her with books. Moreover, he cleared all her doubts, particularly about her vocation. According to him, joy was the proof of the righteousness of any endeavour and, like a compass, it pointed always towards the right direction in life.

Since 1924, a number of Jesuit priests from Yugoslavia had been undertaking missionary work in Calcutta. In the sodality meetings, Father Jambrekovic read enthusiastic and thought-provoking letters and reports from the missionaries there, so that the members would realize the extent of the poverty of the people in Bengal, and that they would be moved to do something for them in the name of God. This is what inspired Agnes to abandon her home and her country for Jesus and to work among the poor.

For six long years Agnes thought and prayed about her vocation. After a while, she was convinced that she was being called to 'belong completely to God'. At first she thought of working among the poor in Africa. However, her great desire soon turned towards serving in India. She made up her mind to leave home and become a missionary when she was eighteen years old. She was convinced by then that her vocation was indeed to work among the poor. She never had any doubt about it, for it was the Lord who had chosen her for this way of life. But the thought of abandoning her mother, brother and sister for good and leaving for a foreign country was very difficult.

Approach Our Holy Mother for anything and everything, was what Nonalok had taught her, and so, for days on end, Agnes knelt in front of the statue of Our Lady of the Black Mountain at Letnice. Each time Our Holy Mother would bring before her mind's eye Her only Son, bearing the crown of thorns, blood weeping from the wounds. She knew that her Lord Jesus shed even the last drop of his blood because of His great love for mankind. It appeared to her as if, thirsting for love, His eyes were inviting her to quench that thirst. She felt as if all the fetters that had fastened her to this world were loosening. An extraordinary strength, and the courage to do anything for the Lord Jesus, was welling up inside her. Eventually, Our Holy Mother herself directed her what to do, 'Abandon all that you have for your Lord Jesus Christ, dedicate yourself entirely to Him, and enter into the life of a nun and serve the poor in Bengal.'

This then became Agnes's great desire and she informed the Jesuit missionaries working in Calcutta of it. They put her in touch with the Loreto nuns, who were working at that time in Bengal; their mother house was in Dublin. To apply to them, she had first to get the permission of her mother, for whom parting with her daughter would be unthinkable. To Nonalok, Agnes was more than a daughter; she was her constant companion and support. Yet, plucking up her courage, Agnes approached her and told her everything with an open heart. Her mother listened patiently and looked at her daughter keenly as if she had never seen her before. Then she went into her room and closed the door behind her, and did not open it for another twenty-four hours.

Most probably she used the same panacea she had often prescribed to Agnes. She must have meditated and thought before Our Holy Mother, and she must have wept, releasing the pain of parting with her child through the channel of her tears. At last she opened the door, came down from the room, embraced Agnes and kissed her repeatedly until they both wept. Then, wiping away their tears, she said, 'My child, offer your hands into the hands of Our Lord Jesus. Accompany Him till your last breath. Live only for God. Our Holy Mother will help you to accomplish what He wants.'

Lazar was a lieutenant in the army of Zog I, the King of Albania. He could not understand or assimilate the idea of his sister becoming a simple nun. Without hiding his displeasure, he wrote her an imperious letter, to which she replied: 'You think you are important, because you are an officer serving a king with two million subjects. However, I am serving the King of the whole world.'

Mother Teresa always remembered the day of her departure from the railway station of Skopje on 26 September 1928. She had wept without restraint, like a baby, in front of

Nonalok, while her friends, relatives and the co-workers of the sodality shed their tears ceaselessly. Her mother and Aga accompanied her as far as Zagreb, and though Agnes was deeply upset, her firm determination to follow Jesus remained steadfast.

At Zagreb, they awaited the arrival of Betika Kajnc, another young woman who wanted to join the Loreto order. When they finally set off on their long train journey across Europe, Agnes waved to Nonalok for the last time. She never saw her beloved mother again – her mother breathed her last in Tirana, Albania, in 1972, without being allowed (by the merciless Communist government) to see her only son Lazar, who was in Sicily, or her loving daughter Agnes, who was of course in India by that time.

On 12 October 1928, Agnes entered Loreto Abbey, Rathfarnham, Dublin, as a postulant. There she stayed for nearly six weeks, spending her time primarily learning English, the language in which she had to accomplish her spiritual studies. She set sail for India on 1 December 1928 and, after a long voyage, she reached Bombay. From there, she took the Bombay mail to Calcutta, where she arrived on 6 January 1929. Her first action was to make a visit to the Blessed Sacrament in St Thomas's Church beside the Loreto Convent, where she offered herself to Jesus in the Blessed Sacrament. When she entered the convent, it was decided she should be sent to Darjeeling on 10 January to begin her novitiate in earnest.

Darjeeling is a hill station 7,000 feet up in the foothills of the Himalayas. The Loreto Convent was situated under the peak of Kanchenjunga and as the young nun approached it for the first time, the mountain was covered with pure white snow. It looked like a symbol of perfect purity. On 23 May 1929, dressed in a black habit and veil, Agnes was formally made a Loreto novice, in the presence and with the blessing of Archbishop Ferdinand Perier.

The novitiate is a period of preparation and probation. Apart from spiritual formation, Loreto nuns had to prepare for their particular apostolate of teaching, and so the young novice spent two years learning Bengali and Hindi. That is why she was later asked to teach in a Bengali school.

Agnes was given the name of Sister Mary Teresa during her novitiate, because the saint who influenced her most at that time was Saint Thérèse of Lisieux, the Little Flower. When Thérèse was canonized, the Holy Father had said, 'She did just ordinary things, with extraordinary love.' Now young Sister Teresa made a strong resolution to do exactly the same. Her friend Betika became Sister Mary Magdalene.

On 24 May 1931, Sister Teresa took her temporary vows of poverty, chastity and obedience, and started teaching in the Loreto School at Darjeeling. She also worked at a small medical station for a short period, helping the nursing staff. One day a man approached her, carrying a bundle with what appeared to be two dry twigs protruding from it. On inspection, she found that they were the emaciated legs of a boy who was on the point of death. Thinking that the nuns would not take the child, the man said, 'If you do not want him, I will throw him into the grass. The jackals will definitely find him useful, won't they?' With great pity and love, the young nun took that poor child, who was totally blind, into her arms and folded him in her apron. Her heart filled with a joy she had never experienced before. Maybe that was the first reward God gave her for saving a soul.

To Sister Teresa, the voice of her superiors was the voice of her Lord Jesus and she obeyed with joy, no matter what. After her novitiate, she was sent from Darjeeling to Loreto Entally in Calcutta, where she was asked to teach moral science, history and geography in St Mary's Bengali Intermediate School. It was at that time she began to be called Bengali Teresa, to distinguish her from another Loreto sister named Teresa. In Calcutta she also taught in St Teresa's Primary School for some time.

Her students were girls belonging to different castes and creeds. She had planned that each class she took must help her, at least to some extent, to lead a good life. With this in mind, she formed a Catholic action group of girls to do some social work. She used to check if she possessed the same qualities she wished to inculcate in her students, for how, she reasoned, can we give anything to someone else, if we do not possess it ourselves? *Nemo dat quod non habet*: 'Nobody can give what they have not got'. She took the girls once or twice a week to visit the poor, diseased and abandoned, to give these unfortunate people all possible help. Reverend Father Julien Henry of St Teresa's Church was kind enough to give them proper guidance. Mother Teresa considered that these visits explained why so many of her students abandoned everything in later years and joined her congregation to serve the poor in the slums.

On 24 May 1937, Sister Teresa took her final vows as a bona fide member of the sisters of Our Lady of Loreto, the congregation founded by Mother Mary Ward in the seventeenth century. At that point she began to be called Mother Teresa, as was the custom for Loreto nuns.

To save the poor was the aim and ambition of Mother Teresa's life. This had formed deep in her mind from early childhood, but she was unable to put it into practice. The best she could do at that point in her life was to help especially those children in her class who were found to be far below the average in wealth as well as in intelligence. Each time she did so, the Omniscient God would reward her with extraordinary mental peace, joy and satisfaction.

Her superiors were satisfied with her teaching skills, making her principal of St Mary's in 1944. She was ready to offer her dedicated service wherever they appointed her, as she considered it a God-given opportunity, but the principalship of St Mary's did not make her mother happy. She wrote to Mother Teresa from Tirana:

My dear child,

Do not forget that you went to India for the sake of the poor.

Do you remember our File? Her body was covered completely with sores. Nevertheless, what caused her far more pain and suffering was the knowledge that she was all alone in the world. We did whatever we could do for her . . .

At that time, God mercifully gave Mother Teresa a great and talented spiritual father – the Belgian Jesuit, Father Celeste Van Exem, an expert in Arabic, Urdu and the Muslim faith. He was living at Baithakana in Calcutta and working with the city's Muslims. Mother Teresa met him on 12 July 1944 and requested him to guide her as her spiritual father. He did not want to busy himself with nuns, nor did he want to be Mother Teresa's spiritual father. Nevertheless, the impossible became possible when God wanted it, and Mother Teresa's spiritual life moved forward thanks to his help.

Father Van Exem infused her with timely courage to do the will of God, to go through the ordeal without fear. On 16 August 1946, a Hindu–Muslim riot erupted in Calcutta. Mother Teresa was in charge of Entally boarding school at the time. No food was available and nearly 300 pupils were hungry. It was her duty to feed them. So she went alone into the streets of Calcutta, where she witnessed the horror of the bloodbath in which hundreds of people were killed and thousands were wounded. Seeing a lonely Loreto nun, the troops were surprised and stopped her. They listened patiently to her story and drove her back to the school with a lorry full of bags of rice.

After 10 September 1946, Mother Teresa's 'inspiration day', Father Van Exem extended a helping hand whenever she was struggling with trials and tribulations. Father Henry also helped her greatly, as spiritual adviser to her and her sisters. However, she was indebted to Father Van Exem in particular for a number of things. He was a canonist and a theologian. It was he who wrote the constitution of the new congregation, who helped obtain the permissions for Mother Teresa from the Archbishop of Calcutta as well as from Rome, who arranged the house of Mr Gomez for the sisters, and who did everything possible to buy the building that turned out later to be the mother house. In short, he was Mother Teresa's greatest support. It was through his inspiration that she began her work at Mothijhil. And it was also through him that the house of miracles came to be.

———

God loved the world so much that He gave His only Son, so that everyone who believes in Him may not die but have eternal life. (John 3:16)

− 2 −

The Voice of Our Lord

The most important day in Mother Teresa's life, she always maintained, was Tuesday, 10 September 1946. On that day, she was travelling by train, in the third-class compartment, from the Loreto Convent in Calcutta to attend a retreat in Darjeeling. After dusk, she began to recite a Rosary, talking silently with Our Holy Mother.

After some time, she took her Bible and opened it gently. 'Open the Holy Book and read', St Augustine was prompted once. However, Mother Teresa never received such direction. 'What does it profit a man if he wins the whole world but loses his immortal soul?' were the sacred words that inspired Francis Xavier and made him a saint, but she did not see those holy words either. What she saw was chapter 25 of the Gospel of St Matthew; beginning at verse 31, she began to read. This is how she described the event:

I felt the holy words piercing into the innermost recesses of my heart, in a way I had never experienced before. You know the story of Saul, who was riding from Jerusalem to Damascus. On the way, a ray of light struck from heaven like lightning; it stopped him, threw him down from his horse and compelled him to listen to the words of Our Lord. I, too, was stopped by the glow of St Matthew's holy words, and was forced to listen to the voice of Our Lord.

She was just thirty-six years old. The cup of her youth was full to the brim with vigour and energy and she knew she could accomplish anything she set out to do. At the time, she did not know that this biblical passage had inspired Tolstoy and Ruskin, and it had induced Francis of Assisi, her beloved saint, to lead a life of selfless service towards his fellow beings. It had encouraged Father Damien to live and work among the rejected and dejected lepers of Molokai, and it had motivated Albert Schweitzer to work amongst the poor and afflicted in Africa.

As the train moved on fast and blew a long whistle, she read the passage again:

When the Son of Man comes as King and all the angels with him, he will sit on his royal throne, and the people of all the nations will be gathered before him. Then he will divide them into two groups, just as a shepherd separates the sheep from the goats. He will put the righteous people on his right and the others on his left.

Then the King will say to the people on his right: 'Come you that are blessed by the Father! Come and possess the kingdom which has been prepared for you ever since the creation of the world.

I was hungry and you fed me, thirsty and you gave me a drink; I was a stranger and you received me in your homes, naked and you clothed me; I was sick and you took care of me, in prison and you visited me.'

The righteous will then ask him: 'When, Lord, did we ever see you hungry and feed you, or thirsty and give you a drink? When did we ever see you a stranger and welcome you in our homes, or naked and clothe you? When did we ever see you sick or in prison, and visit you?'

The King will reply, 'I tell you, whenever you did this for one of the least important of these brothers of mine, you did it for me!'

Then he will say to those on his left, 'Away from me, you that are under God's curse! Away to the eternal fire which has been prepared for the Devil and his angels! I was hungry but you would not feed me, thirsty but you would not give me a drink; I was a stranger but you would not welcome me in your homes, naked but you would not clothe me; I was sick and in prison but you would not take care of me.'

Then they will ask him, 'When, Lord, did we ever see you hungry, or thirsty, or a stranger, or naked or sick or in prison, and we would not help you?'

The King will reply, 'I tell you, whenever you refused to help one of those least important ones, you refused to help me.'

These, then, will be sent off to eternal punishment, but the righteous will go to eternal life.

She closed the Bible, slipped into silence, and became immersed in prayer. Then she heard again the voice of Our Lord quite distinctly.

The plight of the people in Calcutta was never far from her mind and it caused her great turmoil. She had become aware of the miserable life of the poor, the sick and the destitute, and how pitiably the poorest of the poor fell down on the road and breathed their last. This was especially distressing during the notorious Bengal famine of 1942–3. She could not restrain her tears when Father Henry described the misery and misfortune of these people, and when she looked through the windows of her convent, she could see with her own eyes their wretched situation. She would cry out:

The poor human beings!
Who dwell permanently in the jails of poverty!
Who fight with the street dogs in the heap of refuse, just
for some crumbs!
Who perish shivering in the severe cold and hunger
having nothing to wear or to eat!

Who fall down dead vomiting blood due to the ceaseless
cough caused by unattended tuberculosis!
Who die on the roadside like rejected animals due to all
sorts of deprivation, degradation and disease!
Who lie still on the side of the footpath like a dirty bundle
of clothes, expecting death any moment, surrounded
and eaten by ants, maggots and rats!

These heart-rending scenes came back to her now with every
jerk and jolt of the train and her conscience shrieked like the
long whistle of the train:

My dear, don't you see your beloved spouse who dwells in
each one of these unfortunate creatures? Can't you do something for them?

My dear, you must see your beloved Jesus in each one
of these miserable people. You must love that Jesus, serve
that Jesus and look after that Jesus.

Never forget His voice when He says, 'Whenever you
did this for one of the least important brothers of mine,
you did it for me.'

The comforts and conveniences available in the Loreto
Convent in Calcutta were quite meagre, but the voice in her
head urged her to relinquish even that level of comfort and to
go down to the slums and find Jesus in the poor, who suffered
from all sorts of pain and affliction; to look after that Jesus

with her whole heart, with all her might and ability. This was what she always described as her 'inner call' – a second vocation – and it stayed with her throughout her train journey.

Her ambition was to lead a holy life; she wanted to imitate Our Holy Mother; and she wished to proclaim, like her: 'I am the Lord's servant, may it happen to me as He desires' (Luke 1:38). She did not know what she should do exactly, and so she prayed incessantly to Our Holy Mother. At length, during that retreat in Darjeeling, she made a firm resolution to respond to this inner call. The message was quite clear to her. She was to leave the Loreto Convent to live among and help the poor and needy. It was an order. She knew now where she belonged, but she did not know how to get there. Then she happened to read these holy words in the Acts of the Apostles: 'While they were serving the Lord and fasting, the Holy Spirit said to them, "Set apart for me Barnabas and Saul to do the work to which I have called them."' These words opened the eyes of her mind and gave her the courage she had not had before.

But how could she convince her superiors that Our Lord had called her specifically to look after the poor? How could she tell them to set her apart for Our Lord? How could she obtain the necessary permission, as well as the blessing of the Archbishop of Calcutta and of her Mother Superior, to leave Loreto?

These impossible matters were settled by her beloved Lord Jesus.

– 3 –

The Crosses of Obstruction

When the retreat in Darjeeling came to an end, Mother Teresa returned to Calcutta with the inner call she had received from God that day on the train. She shared some of her plans about this second vocation with a few close friends at Loreto, but they were afraid even to imagine such a young nun going alone from the convent to help the poor in the slums. Nevertheless, she revealed the whole plan to her Mother Superior and to Archbishop Perier. Contrary to her expectations, neither gave her a favourable reply or positive assurance. So she turned to Father Van Exem, submitting to him two sheets of paper on which she had noted down all that had happened between her and Jesus, the entire details of her second vocation. But, at first, Father Van Exem gave her no encouragement either.

Mother Teresa was always ready to do anything and to suffer anything for Jesus, but how could she get out of the convent without the explicit permission of her Mother

Superior? The door seemed closed for ever. Indeed, even she wondered if it was proper for a young nun like herself to go out into the streets and slums of Calcutta alone. Was it fitting for her to establish a new field of work or a new congregation? Mother Superior certainly considered both these things to be most improper; what was proper, in her view, was to commit the young nun to another post as soon as possible.

And so she quickly transferred Mother Teresa from Calcutta to Asansol, believing that the transfer would extinguish the spirit burning in her. Teresa obeyed, left for Asansol and took up her new assignment, offering the chalice of her agony to Our Holy Mother, weeping and repeating the words of Our Lord, 'Not my will, but thy will be done' (Luke 22:42). Before long, she began to experience the intervention of Our Holy Mother. The Archbishop of Calcutta informed the Mother Superior that he was not happy with the transfer of Mother Teresa to Asansol at that juncture, and later he insisted that Mother Teresa should be posted back to Calcutta again.

At that time, the struggle for freedom in India was everywhere reaching new heights. On Mother Teresa's return to Calcutta, her first task was to calm the waves of unrest spreading among the girls in the school in which she worked. Placing all her trust in the Lord Jesus, who had calmed the violent storm and the troubled sea, she met the leaders of the girls one by one. Patiently, she listened to whatever they had to say. She talked amiably to them, individually and in company with others. They found it difficult to ignore her loving and sincere request and within a short time, the tumult settled down, order and peace were restored, and the school began to function normally again. She thanked Jesus, not just for the return of peace to the school, but also because her influence in resolving these problems became one of the reasons her superiors granted her permission to work among the poor in the slums.

Once again she urged Father Van Exem to obtain Archbishop Perier's permission for her work in Calcutta. At that time the congressmen, inspired by Mahatma Gandhi, were doing all sorts of social service among the poor, work that was receiving great appreciation and acceptance in and around the city. As Father Henry had considerable experience in working among the poor in the slums, Father Van Exem brought him with him when he approached the archbishop on Mother Teresa's behalf. They tried their best to convince him that there was no harm in giving permission to Mother Teresa to work among the poor, but the more the archbishop thought about it, the more reluctant he became to grant this request. He considered it to be a risk. His final verdict was, 'This is not an apt time for a European lady to go down into the slums or streets of Calcutta, to work among the poor. So let's wait at least for another year before we begin that gamble.' Instead, he suggested to Mother Teresa that she should live and work with the Daughters of St Anne, a religious congregation under his jurisdiction, who dressed like Indian women, ate simple food, slept in dormitories, lived like the poor, and worked for the poor. 'Just give it a try,' he urged. He knew that the Vatican did not encourage the multiplication of religious orders for women. A bishop applying for the approbation of a new religious order in his diocese had to prove that none of the existing houses could do the work of the new order. And so Mother Teresa lived and worked with the Daughters of St Anne for some time. However, it was as clear as day to her that the Lord Jesus had not given her her second vocation for this sort of life and, by this time, Father Van Exem had no doubt about it either.

So Father Van Exem met the archbishop again and threw more light on a letter Mother Teresa had written to His Grace, explaining that her intention, according to her second vocation, was to work not only among the poor, but specifically among the *very poorest of the poor*, giving them whatever she had. The archbishop eventually decided to grant her permission but with a proviso. With his approval, Mother Gertrude, the Mother General of the Loreto order, authorized Mother Teresa to write to Rome, asking for permission to leave the convent.

In February 1948, Archbishop Perier sent her letter to His Holiness Pope Pius XII:

Holy Father,

This humble servant has a 'call within the call' according to which I am relinquishing everything I have and offering myself for the service of the poorest of the poor in slums.

I humbly request Your Holiness to grant me the necessary permission for it as well as the blessing . . .

The archbishop enclosed a covering letter, providing details of Teresa's life and work. On 12 April, the Holy Father sent a decree through the apostolic nuncio at Delhi, granting permission. It was not until 8 August, however, that Mother Teresa was allowed to leave Loreto for one year, when her right to continue her work would be dependent on the 'good pleasure' of the archbishop. Just after Holy Mass on Sunday, Father Van Exem called her to the bishop's parlour to give her the good news: 'Teresa, you have the decree of exclaustration for one year. You can start doing the work . . . You are no longer a Loreto nun.' Her heart filled with joy and she thanked God.

Saying goodbye to Loreto for good was very difficult for Mother Teresa. It was the greatest sacrifice she was asked to make, the hardest thing she had ever done. It was more difficult than leaving her family and her country to enter the religious life. Loreto, where she had received her spiritual training, where she had worked for a long time and where she had given herself to Jesus, meant everything to her. Yet she left Loreto to serve the poor and the destitute. As she would say herself, *Thank God*.

On 18 August 1948, the gate of the Loreto Convent closed behind her for good. For the first time in her life, she said, she felt that she was just like a small boat without a boatman, in the midst of the wild waves of a vast lake. She had nobody to support her, no place to call her own, no money, no job and no one to depend on. For the first time in her life, she experienced the miserable feelings of an orphan. With tears in her eyes, she told Jesus, 'Lord, you, you alone are my support. I trust in your call. You will not let me down.' And then she sang, like the psalmist, 'I place all my trust in you my Lord. All my hope is in your mercy.' The following words of Our Lord then came to her mind, 'I assure you that if you have faith as big as a mustard seed, you can say to this mountain, "Go from here to there" and it will go. You can do anything' (Matthew 17:20).

The gate to life is narrow and the way that leads to it is hard, and there are few people who find it. (Matthew 7:14)

– 4 –

Caring for the Poor

Mother Teresa had been a teacher and she had neither the necessary knowledge nor sufficient experience to look after the poor. However, she had heard about a nursing school run by the Medical Mission sisters at the Holy Family Hospital in Patna beside the River Ganges. Through the help of Archbishop Perier, she was admitted to the school to acquire some medical training, and so, on 18 August 1948, she left for Patna.

She relinquished the official habit of the Loreto nun that she had worn for nearly twenty years and she put on the simple white sari with a blue border, worn by women working as scavengers in Calcutta, who made daily house-to-house visits, collecting the excreta and carrying it away. Mother Teresa thought this sari would be the most suitable uniform for her and her sisters. Is it not better to wear the dress of the poor if we are intending to serve the poor? she thought to herself. 'Yes,' said Our Lord, the God who became a man to redeem mankind. Father Van Exem blessed and gave her three such saris. Mother Teresa was to find a new symbol and meaning for that dress: for her the white sari came to represent holiness and the blue border stood for Our Holy Mother, and later it became the uniform of the sisters of the Missionaries of Charity. Just as Bengali women keep the keys of their houses well tied up on one end of their sari, so Mother Teresa tied a small crucifix to one end of her sari.

The blessing of God, together with Mother Teresa's enthusiasm and eagerness, meant that she acquired an adequate medical knowledge at the nursing school, and she mastered, within a short time, all that was necessary to minister to the sick and afflicted. She gained enough experience to look after newborn babies, to diagnose common illnesses, to prescribe some medicines, to give urgent injections and offer suitable medical attention to those who had met with accidents.

As soon as she had learned all she needed, Mother Teresa wished to return to Calcutta, but Father Van Exem and the archbishop were not willing to allow her to begin her work in the slums without at least six months' training. Father Van Exem came to Patna, met Sister Stephanie, the Superior of the Medical Mission sisters, and one of the sister doctors under whom Mother Teresa was a trainee, to discuss the matter with them. Sister Stephanie told him that she was confident Teresa had acquired enough medical training to work in the slums.

Meanwhile, Teresa had found favour with Mother Dengel, the foundress of the Medical Mission sisters, who had, with great difficulty, obtained permission from the Holy See for her nuns to practise surgery and midwifery in their hospitals. Mother Teresa had disclosed to her her future plans: 'The sisters of the congregation I intend to start,' she said, 'will lead the lives of India's poor. They will dress and eat like the poorest of the poor whom they will feed, clothe and tend. The poor in India hardly get rice and dal for their meals; but we will be satisfied just with rice and salt.' Mother Dengel, who had much appreciation for Teresa's second vocation and for her new programme, gave her a broad smile and said:

Sister Teresa, your intentions are good. However, the manner in which you wish to execute them seems to be inadequate and improper. The sisters must eat enough, not only to survive but also to serve others. If they work without proper nutrition, it is impossible for them to work efficiently. Moreover, they will become the victims of the same disease, tuberculosis, that afflicts the poor. So, you should not tempt Jesus to work miracles daily for you, to keep up the health of the members of your congregation.

Mother Teresa considered this advice to be the command of Our Lord. Yet, in her mind she could see only the miserable way the poor lived. Do they have proper clothes? she thought. Enough food? A place to dwell? Do they have a fan, a fridge, a washing machine, or any other modern facility that even the ordinary people enjoy in this century? If not, then why should the sisters have them?

In Calcutta there was a congregation of the Little Sisters of the Poor, founded by Jeanne Jugan, a French nun. They were committed to poverty and depended on what they received from begging. They looked after nearly 200 old people in their St Joseph's Home. Mother Teresa lived in a small room on the first floor of that holy home for some time when she returned from her medical training in Patna. From St Joseph's, she used to go out to the slums each morning after Mass and breakfast to attend the poor, sick and miserable destitutes, who were in a worse situation than the old people in the home, living on the roadside and with no one to depend on.

Mother Teresa felt that the dress of an Indian woman alone was not sufficient to allow her to work for Indians, and so she became an Indian citizen that year. India is a great country: there is economic poverty but the minds of thousands of India's poor are immensely rich. Mother Teresa wanted to live with them and like them. That is why she became an Indian. 'It is the poor of India made me what I am,' she used to say. 'I am indebted to them. My life and soul are in the midst of these people.'

Acting on the advice of Father Van Exem, Mother Teresa made a retreat from 10–18 December 1948. On the morning of the 21st, wearing her blue-bordered, white sari, she went to

St Teresa's presbytery, where Father Henry was living. She wondered whether he would recognize her. He looked at her curiously, gave her a beautiful smile, and then nodded his head, saying, 'Of course, Mother Teresa. Where are you going to?'

'Mothijhil,' she told him.

Mothijhil was an area of Calcutta just beyond the wall of the school where she had been teaching for a long time, about three miles from St Joseph's Home. 'Mothijhil' means 'lake of pearls', but instead of pearls there was just a pool of dirty water, surrounded by foul smelling, filthy slums, which seemed to contain all sorts of illness, poverty, ignorance, dejection and degradation. Teresa approached this place, closing her nostrils every now and then. She found a few naked children wandering like sheep without a shepherd. She smiled sweetly at them and spoke softly, showering them with ceaseless love, and soon she had persuaded them to let her give them a bath. It was the first time they had ever seen a cake of soap. Their parents were scavengers or sweepers working for Calcutta Corporation and they lived in filth, in small huts. Everywhere was the noise of coughing, weeping or lamenting. There was not a single hut that didn't have at least one sick person. 'Is not the darkness of ignorance the cause of all this?' Mother Teresa asked herself. She decided that she must first chase away that darkness, and light the lamp of knowledge.

And so she called all the children that happened to be

around her. Four or five of them responded. Then she said a prayer and started teaching them the Bengali alphabet. Instead of chalk, she used a piece of stick, and instead of a blackboard, she used the wet ground. She found a little vacant place between the huts. There, under a guava tree, she started her primary class. When the class was over, she visited the huts, met the patients in them, enquired after them and consoled them.

She heard that there was a vacant room available in the area, so she enquired about the rent. Five rupees a month, she was told. That room became her classroom. The number of students began to increase until it reached thirty-five. She taught them the alphabet, how to wash and comb their hair, and how to keep themselves clean and clothed. She taught them that they are children of God, who loves them very much. Soon they learned the first lessons of cleanliness and hygiene and they began to attend the class regularly. Mother Teresa would give them a cake of soap as a present for cleanliness, regularity and attention. She also managed later to give them a little milk at noon. The total amount of cash that she had to begin her work may have been only five rupees, but the holy words 'The Lord is my shepherd, and there is nothing I shall want' used to give her courage.

People began to notice what she was doing. Though they were poor, they presented her with all that was required, without her having to ask for it. One after the other, blackboard, chalk, chair and table appeared in her classroom. Then Father Vicar of Park Circus gave her 100 rupees, which allowed her to rent a second room. Now she had one room for her class and the other for her dispensary, which also served as the first home for the sick and dying destitute. On the second day, some of Mother Teresa's former students came down to Mothijhil and helped her in her work. Later, a few teachers, former colleagues, joined her. They were sympathetic to her and the work she was doing, as she was their former principal. Seeing her work under such pathetic conditions, they took pity on her. But they did not choose to remain and work with her permanently.

Mother Teresa's diary from that time reveals what occupied her mind:

I saw Master X on Friday. He came to school starving, as he had nothing at home to eat. I had with me three annas [one-sixteenth of a rupee] just for my return journey by tram. I gave it to him, and asked him to buy something and eat. In the evening, I returned to my dwelling on foot. Today I learned a good lesson.

Our Lord wants me to be a free nun covered with the poverty of the Cross. The poverty of the poor must be so hard for them. While looking for a home, I walked and walked till my legs ached. I thought how much they must ache in body and soul, looking for a home, food and health.

Then the comfort of Loreto came to tempt her: 'You have only to say the word and that will be yours again,' the Tempter repeated. Teresa prayed to God, 'Of free choice, my God, and out of love for You, I desire to remain and do whatever may be Your holy will in my regard.'

She did not let a single tear fall, but she prayed to Our Lord to give her strength to fulfil His will. 'The poor people are to be educated,' she told herself. 'The sick are to be looked after. The destitute are to be sheltered. The conviction that everyone is a child of God is to be impressed on the minds of all. Living in the midst of the poor, I am to give them whatever they want. They are to be helped and uplifted. It is to accomplish this task that Our Lord gave me a call within the call.'

Still, she had negative thoughts also: 'Nothing is possible for me. Nothing. I am utterly useless, like a bottomless bucket. I am good for nothing.' She cried to Jesus from the whirlpool of despair and desolation. And she cried to Our Lord:

My God, You, only You. I trust in Your call, in your inspiration. You will not let me down. Lord, You are my strength, You alone. My being and all that I think to be mine belong to You. Use me and make me worthy of any use. Is it not You who turned me out of Loreto? Was I not of some use inside that convent? But now, be with me. I can't do anything without You. I can't see anything. I am groping in the darkness. Lord, lead me into light. Lead me as You like.

She cried desperately. How did Our Lord wipe away her tears? How did He help her? How did He save her from drowning in the sea of despair? You shall hear.

———

The Lord is my shepherd, There is nothing I shall want. (Psalm 23:1)

– 5 –

When the Almighty Provides

In February 1949, Mother Teresa had to find somewhere to live. She started searching but found nothing. She was wandering for days on end and her feet were aching, and for the first time in her life she realized the anxiety and agony of the poor who had no house of their own to sleep in at night. She was certain that the Almighty, who drew her out of Loreto, would definitely provide her with a suitable dwelling place, but she also had to put in her share of humble efforts, and so she asked Father Van Exem to try to find her some accommodation. Father Henry was also kind enough to help her, and both men rode on their bicycles along the streets of Calcutta, in search of a small house for this poor nun.

One day Father Van Exem gave her the good news, 'Mother Teresa, I have found a suitable home for you, on the top floor of the house of Mr Michael Gomez.'

When Mother Teresa went along to see the house at 14 Greek Lane, she could not suppress her surprise. It seemed too big, of too high a standard, and hence most unsuitable for poor nuns.

'Whatever may be,' Father Henry said, 'think that it is what Our Lord decides to grant you at the moment.'

After that, Teresa did not hesitate. She had prayed to Jesus for a hut, and what he gave her was a palace! The next day, 28 February, she moved in, and Charur Ma, a widow who was working in St Mary's school, moved in with her. Mr Gomez was a generous man and charged her no rent, and from that day on, Mother Teresa had a sweet companion to go with her every day to the slums – Mabel, his eight-year-old daughter.

Mother Teresa's next problem was where to get the many medicines she urgently needed for the poor. She was ready to beg, and Mr Gomez was kind enough to accompany her, and so they went to a large medical shop. She submitted a list to the manager and requested him in a humble tone, 'Sir, I shall be much obliged if you kindly supply me these medicines for the poor. It will be a great help for them. I have no money.'

The manager threw the list on his table, stared at the little nun for a moment, and then shouted at her angrily, 'Woman, you are making a big mistake. This is not the place where you get medicines free. This is the place where we *sell* medicines. Understand? I have got plenty of other work to do. Won't you allow me to do it peacefully?'

She made no reply. Mr Gomez too remained quiet. But Teresa prayed to God to bless abundantly the manager who scolded her and humiliated her with his harsh words. Placing all her trust in Our Holy Mother, she sat outside the shop, and she recited a Rosary silently.

The manager had a change of heart and to the surprise of the nun and her companion, he looked at her as gently and amiably as a little lamb and uttered in a meek and pleasing voice, 'Please look at these three parcels on the table. They are the medicines you asked for. Please accept them as a gift from our company.'

'Thank you very much, sir,' Mother Teresa replied. 'God bless you and your company.'

She always had faith that she could get whatever she needed through the intercession of Our Holy Mother and, indeed, she obtained innumerable favours in this way. 'As St Bernard says,' she would claim, 'if we pray to Our Holy Mother, as a child does to its mother, earnestly and repeatedly, she will never reject us. You may try too and see if you have any doubt about it.'

One day, before she started living in Mr Gomez's house, someone called at her home. She could not believe her eyes when she opened the door, for there was Subhashini Das, one of her former students at St Mary's. When she joined the school at the age of nine, Mother Teresa was her class teacher. Teresa welcomed her in with open arms.

Subhashini said, 'Mother, I have come to live with you.'

Subhashini was the first young woman who wanted to join Mother Teresa's new congregation. She had been a member of the sodality at Loreto and used to accompany Mother Teresa on her visits to the poor and the sick. She had all the qualities required to become an excellent nun. But, nevertheless, Mother Teresa was concerned.

'What!' she said. 'Look at these rough hands of mine and at my simple and cheap sari. Compare them with those of yours and then tell me, how is it possible for you to lead such a simple life? You would have to forget yourself. You need to practise self-denial, surrender and devote yourself entirely to God and our fellow beings. Get ready to suffer any sort of sacrifice. Then and then only—'

'Mother,' Subhashini interrupted, 'I am ready. I have thought it over at length and am prepared for it.'

Mother Teresa had a great desire to take her young friend in, but she sacrificed it for the sake of Jesus for the time being. She urged Subhashini to go back and think a little more seriously, to pray to Jesus, for a few days. After all, she could not even offer her accommodation, though she was sure that Jesus would give them all they needed at the right time.

'You are welcome to join me,' she said, 'but not now, not until we have a house. So please go and come back after a few days. I shall pray for you.'

Subhashini left, like an obedient student. Days passed. On 19 March, on the feast of St Joseph, Mother Teresa was praying in her room. Subhashini came again and knocked at her door. Teresa was again surprised to see her, for Subhashini looked completely changed. She had no ornaments. Even the clothes she wore were of the cheapest kind. These were the clear signs of her self-sacrifice.

She said, 'Mother, here I am. Please don't ask me to go back. My decision to join you came from the very bottom of my heart.'

And so Mother Teresa embraced her with motherly affection and satisfaction and welcomed her to the house of Mr Gomez, which God's providence had arranged for them. From that day, Subhashini was the first and the best among the sisters of the Missionaries of Charity. Agnes was the name that she received when she became a sister. Until her last breath, she was at Mother Teresa's right hand. She was the first novice mistress and she was the sister who, during Mother Teresa's absences, took upon her shoulders all the responsibilities of the convent and executed them excellently. On 9 April 1997, when Sister Agnes was suffering from cancer and dying in Calcutta, God gave Mother Teresa the grace to be at her bedside, to attend and console her during the last minutes of her agony.

But on that day in 1949, she thanked Jesus for giving her Subhashini. In front of the altar, she knelt down and told Jesus, present in the Holy Sacrament, 'My beloved Jesus, how good You are! So, You are sending them one by one to my humble group, keeping the promise You made to me. Thank you, thank you, Jesus, for Your goodness.'

One day she heard that a Muslim woman was seriously sick. She took some medicines from the dispensary at

Mothijhil, went to her hut, gave her the necessary medication and consoled and comforted her. The sick woman gave her a beautiful smile of gratitude and said, 'I have been suffering severe pain for the past several years. Only today, for the first time, I don't feel any pain at all. It is Allah who sent you to me!'

Another aged Muslim woman folded her hands and begged, 'Mother, would you please give me your consent just for one thing? When I become seriously ill and almost sinking, could you please come and sit near me? I want to die being very close to Allah. That is my only great desire.'

There were several old people and children in Mothijhil who were in need of love and consolation, like that old woman. Mother Teresa used to send patients suffering from meningitis, cholera, tetanus and other serious diseases, whom she was unable to treat herself, to the Campbell Hospital (now the Nilrathan Sarkar Hospital). Whenever she asked for the ambulance, the authorities were always ready to send it.

Mother Teresa had taught Sister Rosario her first lessons in Bengali, in Loreto. When Sister Rosario became the principal of St Mary's, she was kind enough to grant Mother Teresa a small room in the parish school to set up a dispensary. After school hours, Sister Rosario also allowed her to use the school veranda as a temporary dispensary, especially for undernourished people who were suffering from tuberculosis. Most of the people were poor rickshaw-pullers and carriers of head loads, and other hard-working people who had no means of getting any sort of treatment. Mother Teresa couldn't possibly say no to Jesus, who was present in each one of them. It was her duty to serve them and she managed somehow to treat them, procuring the necessary medicines from somewhere.

Mr Gomez tells the following story:

One day I was travelling to Howrah by tram along with Mother Teresa. India had by then become an independent country. The people were enjoying their hard-earned freedom, whenever and wherever they met. Besides, that was the time they used to ruminate over the suppression and oppression the Indians had to undergo, having been in the fetters of foreign rule.

The people in the tram saw Mother Teresa wearing a white sari like a Bengali woman. Yet, they could see that she was a foreigner, so they commented despicably in Bengali: 'What is the business of the foreigners in free India now? Are they not staying here to convert the Hindus to Christianity? All the foreigners should be packed off to their own countries.' They thought that Mother did not know Bengali, and they abused her and laughed at her in their own language.

Mother did not know her fundamental rights as an Indian. India is a secular country where every person has a constitutional right to believe in any religion and to propagate any religion. Yet, she looked at those who were insulting her with tolerance and forgiveness. Then she said calmly but quite clearly in pure Bengali: '*Ami*

Bharather, Bharath Amar.' Which means, I am an Indian and India is my country.

It was a surprise for the people sitting in the tram. They heard it with great astonishment. Soon they felt sorry and ashamed of their unkind talk and behaviour. As a result, none of them opened their mouths to speak till they reached Howrah.

On 29 May 1949, Teresa wrote a letter to a friend in Europe:

You will be glad to hear that at present I have got three companions – great and zealous workers. We have different slums where we go for a few hours. What suffering! What a hunger for God! Yet, we are so few to carry Our Lord to them. You should see their eager faces, how their faces brighten up when the sisters approach them. Dirty and naked though they may be, their hearts are full of love and affection. I trust in your prayers. Ask Our Lady to give us more sisters. In Calcutta itself, we would have full work even if we were twenty.

In November 1949, she wrote again to her friend:

Pray much that the little society may grow in sanctity and numbers, if it is the will of God. Yes, there is so much to be done; at present we are five. But, please God, more will join, and then we will be able to make a ring of charity round Calcutta, using our centres in the different slums as points, from where the love of Our Lord may freely radiate on the great city of Calcutta.

You will be glad to know that at Boitakhana we have a Sunday Mass for poor slum children. We bring the poor children and their mothers to church. We have up to 120 mothers and 300 children. We started last May with only twenty-six children.

At the dispensary, the Catholic doctors and nurses are wonderful. The way they look after the people, you would think they were the princes of the country. Their charity is wonderful and beautiful.

In the slums you can now hear the children sing. Their faces brighten up with smiles when the sisters come. Their parents, too, do not ill-treat their children. This is just what I have been longing to see among the poor. *Thank God.*

Nowadays it is possible to treat and cure tuberculosis and leprosy. There are effective drugs for both. There are now medicines and cures for all kinds of diseases. However, Mother Teresa used to say, 'The worst possible disease that can affect a human being is his feeling that he is utterly useless and unwanted in his society.' She believed that, to cure this serious disease, all that is required are willing hands to serve and loving hearts to love. She set out to find the dejected, depressed and unwanted people and to find Jesus in every one of them, to perceive in them that Jesus who cries, 'I thirst just for a drop of the water of love.'

———

Be concerned, above everything else, with the kingdom of God and with what He requires of you; and He will provide you with all these other things. (Matthew 6:33)

– 6 –

Quenching the Thirst

Mother Teresa used to say:

> I can see and hear Jesus, who weeps and cries aloud bitterly 'I thirst', on every footpath and from every slum. It is the same Jesus I see in the Blessed Sacrament. I see Jesus there, in the form of bread. I see the same Jesus here in the slums, in the broken bodies and in the rejected children, who also cry, 'I thirst'. Not one or two – but a multitude of persons! How can I remain deaf or inactive? How can I go away without giving Him at least a single drop of love to quench His thirst? However, how can I do it alone when the cries are innumerable?

The Lord Almighty came to Mother Teresa's help: following Sister Agnes, He began to send young well-educated and dedicated women, one after the other. Magdalene Gomez, a former student of Mother Teresa's at St Mary's, became Sister

Gertrude, the first doctor in the congregation, who would treat and take care of the poor so well. Agnes Vincent, another former student of Mother Teresa's, became Sister Florence, and soon there appeared Sister Dorothy, Sister Margaret and so on – altogether seven nuns. In fact, ten of the first twelve Missionaries of Charity sisters were former students of Mother Teresa's. She thanked Jesus for every one of them.

All the sisters experienced true poverty. There were times when they had to work very hard all day and had to be satisfied with raw wheat and cold water for supper. None of them ever complained. The God of Love and Mercy, who never failed to see how they strained to quench His thirst, not only consoled them but also, at times, used to enthral them, with an extraordinary shower of blessings. One evening, after the day's work was done, Mother Teresa and her, by now, fifteen sisters were as hungry as any miserable poor person who was starving the whole day.

'What shall I do, my Lord?' Teresa prayed.

And at once the Lord prompted her to write a short letter. Sister Claire delivered it to Mr Dominic, a gentleman from Goa who was running a bakery nearby. He accepted the letter as if he were receiving money, and immediately sent two pounds of bread free of charge. Our Lord was taking a special interest to put out the fire of poverty that Mother Teresa and her sisters had fallen into during the inception of the congregation.

Another evening, for example, they had enough rice to cook for their supper. But what could be done when the poor, who had not had a single grain of rice for days, approached them? Willingly and gladly, they distributed among these people all that they had and were ready to go to bed without supper. But Mother Teresa thought how all the young women who joined her congregation had come from wealthy families. They had never experienced starvation before they joined her. She felt sorry for sending them to bed without giving them anything to eat after a hard day's work, so she went to the chapel and with tears in her eyes, told this to Jesus, and returned to her room well consoled.

After some time, there was a knock on her door, and when she opened it, she saw a stranger with a bag in her hand.

'What can I do for you?' Mother Teresa asked with a smile, though she had nothing to give her.

To Teresa's surprise and great satisfaction, the stranger smiled back and said, 'Mother, in this bag, I have some rice for you; would you please accept it?'

She received it with thanks. It was suppertime, and so she took the small tin cup the nuns used to measure out rice and found she had been given exactly the measure of rice they needed for that day.

Then there was the day in Shishu Bhavan in Delhi. There was little food for the poor children and the nuns liked to give them at least some dal along with the simple rice. However, they had no money to buy dal, and so all they had to give the hungry children was rice with a little salt. To their surprise, they saw a car, from the house of Prime Minister

Indira Gandhi, coming towards Shishu Bhavan at speed. It halted at the gate and while the sisters stared open-mouthed, the door of the car opened slowly. What came out of the car were different kinds of vegetables – just what they needed to give to the poor children along with the rice! They were very fresh, as they had only just been picked from the kitchen garden, and it was Mrs Sonia Gandhi who had urged the driver to make sure they reached Shishu Bhavan before noon. On that day, the poor children of Shishu Bhavan in Delhi, as well as the sisters who looked after them, enjoyed a good meal. For this and other instances of the wonderful providence of God, Mother Teresa was always grateful to Our Lord.

One December, a newcomer to the congregation arrived in Calcutta. It was so cold that it was impossible for her to sleep without bedding, so the nuns collected the few materials available and started making bedding for her, but they ran short of cotton before they had stitched half of it. Immediately, Mother Teresa went inside and brought her pillow, telling the sisters to make use of the cotton in it to complete the bedding. They were reluctant to do so, as they did not want to let Mother Teresa sleep without a pillow. After some time, someone rang the doorbell. Mother Teresa opened the door to a young man from Europe. She smiled as usual, wished him good evening and asked him, 'What can I do for you, my son?'

'Mother,' he said, 'could you please do me a favour?'

Mother Teresa agreed that she would.

'Mother, I am leaving for England tomorrow and so I have brought along with me this small cotton bedding. I thought that it could be of some use for somebody here. Would you please accept it?'

He gave Mother Teresa the cotton bedding folded under his arm. She accepted it with many thanks. He talked with her for a minute; and it turned out that the young man had not planned to give the nuns the bedding until the next day, but at the moment that Mother Teresa had decided to give away her pillow, which gave her some comfort at night, he changed his mind. He became an agent that helped his bedding to get to the convent! If we give away anything in the name of God, Mother Teresa would explain, He, the Omniscient, reciprocates with such love, care and interest, and rewards us, sometimes immediately.

One day Mr Kushwant Singh accompanied Mother Teresa to a biscuit factory. They boarded a crowded tram and, immediately, a young man stood up and offered her his seat. Another stood up, untied a knot in his dhoti and took out change to buy the nun a ticket, but the ticket conductor refused to take money. Instead, he punched a ticket for her, which he paid for himself.

When they reached the biscuit factory, Mr Mukherjee, the manager, felt embarrassed. His spirits fell. Every year at Christmas he gave Mother Teresa forty tins of discarded broken biscuits for the poor children. But this year he was unable to do so. The factory had not been functioning properly, due to union problems, and how can there be biscuits in a closed factory? He told them his problems one by one. Finally he said he was sorry for sending them away empty-handed. While she tried to console him, he picked up his phone and asked the store-keeper, 'Have you collected any broken biscuits to give to Mother Teresa?' He expected a negative answer.

Hearing the reply, Mr Mukherjee was much surprised. With a broad smile he said, 'Mother, forty tins of broken biscuits had already been collected long before the union trouble started. You can have them.'

Mother Teresa thanked him, and she thanked God too. 'Don't be surprised,' she told the astonished Mr Mukherjee, 'the Omniscient God had arranged for this year too, the ration you always give me every year for Christmas for our poor children. *Thank God.*'

There was a time when the nuns had not enough money even for the bare necessities of life. The number of members in the congregation was increasing, yet what could they do if they found another person much more in need of money and materials than they were?

People in India and abroad donated to Mother Teresa all that they had, making a big sacrifice and often disregarding their own necessities. Children sent her their pocket money. A boy once refused to use sugar for a few days and the money he saved was donated to her for the poor. Even a beggar came to Teresa and gave her all that he had been given that day. She knew that he would be starving later, but his agony would be much more intolerable if she did not accept it. 'There is no one on earth who ruined himself because he had given away what he had to the poor,' she would say. 'There is no one on earth who has received no peace and happiness because he gave with pain alms to the poor.' And reflecting on a lifetime of experience, she would often say, 'You can be sure that whoever gives even a drink of cold water to one of the least important persons in my name will certainly receive a reward.' (Matthew 10:42)

When they were feeding and looking after thousands of poor people a day, they were usually receiving enough financial aid from India and abroad to do this service. One day, however, the sister in charge of feeding the poor came to Mother Teresa early in the morning and said, 'Mother, what shall we do? Soon the poor will be lining up for food, but we don't have anything to give them. How can I tell them that there is no food for them today or tomorrow?'

Mother Teresa couldn't think of a reply, but she well remembered how the Lord Jesus fed and satisfied 5,000 people by multiplying five loaves of bread and two fishes. Is there anything impossible for Him? 'Excluding children, we have to feed nearly 7,000 people. Show us some way or other, my Lord,' she prayed to Jesus, placing all her trust in Him.

As the clock struck nine, baskets of loaves began to reach the convent! At first, nobody knew where they came from, but then one of the people carrying the baskets stopped and explained that these were loaves that were to be distributed among the schoolchildren but, according to a decision taken by the government, all the schools in the area were closed on that day, and so they were ordered to take the loaves to the nuns. More than 7,000 people ate them for two days, and still there were several baskets of loaves left over.

Always, Mother Teresa would have stories like this of how she had been a living witness to incidents that reveal the wonderful providence of God.

Usually she and her sisters would go out and beg and would then live on whatever they collected. They didn't want to own anything. If they required something, they would choose and buy the cheapest item. They wanted to live in abject poverty, because it made it easier for them to know, love and serve the poor better. Mother Teresa maintained that the poor people of India were more generous than she was. One night somebody came to her to report that there was a poor Hindu family with eight children living near by. They were all starving, as it had been several days since they had eaten as much as a grain of rice. Immediately, she took all the rice she had. It was not much, but enough for their supper. She went to the home of the starving family, and the mother of the house received the rice with great joy. She thanked Mother Teresa and she thanked God. Then she took half of that rice and hastened away, saying that she would be back soon.

When she came back, Mother Teresa asked her, 'Where did you go in such a hurry? What did you do?'

'Mother,' she said, 'I went to my next-door neighbour. They are Muslims. They have the same number of children as we have. They are all starving like us. So, I gave them half of the rice you gave me.'

Looking into their smiling eyes, Mother Teresa could see the love of God glowing. From that glow she learned what Our Lord had taught us – love thy neighbour as thyself – and she remembered that her own beloved mother had once also given to the poor half of the food they were about to eat. We can bring heaven on earth, she would say, if we try to imitate people like this. There is more than enough food in this world for all of us to eat, if we only share it.

Once, a patient who had been bedridden for twenty-five years due to severe illness gave Mother Teresa a donation of fifteen dollars. He was able to move only his right hand and even that was with much difficulty. The only consolation he had, occasionally, was smoking. He wrote: 'Mother, I stopped smoking for a week; and herewith I am sending you the money I would have spent on it.' Fifteen dollars – not at all a big amount, but it represented so much self-denial and sacrifice. With that money, she bought some loaves of bread and distributed them among the wretched who were starving. It not only fed and comforted them, but also filled her with comfort and joy. There is much joy in giving, was her constant belief, and the joy increases without limits when we give with pain, arising out of great sacrifice.

She used to teach the sisters how to deal with the poor,

'See Jesus in each one of them; touch that Jesus tenderly and devotedly as you touch Jesus in the Holy Sacrament; and serve that Jesus whole-heartedly and with all your ability.' Not only did she exhort them to behave in this way, but she also exhibited to them through her own actions how to be with the poor, the sick and the afflicted. At times, they would arrive in a terrible state, filthy, covered with sores and ulcers, eaten up by syphilis, cancer or leprosy. The nuns would wash them all, but the worst cases Mother Teresa would attend to herself, praying to God:

> God, Our Father, as You and Your Son Jesus Christ are united to be one, make us sisters all united as one; and help us to live in Your spirit. As You love us we must also love one another and we must transmit, channel and pass on that love to the poor we come across; and for this, dear Lord, please come and live in each and every one of us.

It was exactly what her mother had taught her in childhood and she, in turn, taught her sisters.

––––––

He gives food to every living creature; his love is eternal, give thanks to the God of Heaven. (Psalm 136:25)

– 7 –

House of Miracles

'On the streets of Calcutta,' Mother Teresa would often say, 'you may find discarded human beings – abandoned parents, discarded children, most of them unconscious or motionless, all poor destitutes that no one wants. Suffering from starvation, disease and deprivation, they are dying by the wayside, like insects trapped in the fire.'

However, there is a house in Calcutta where such people are taken in and tended carefully, treated like gods, given whatever they need, and inundated with mercy, love and care beyond measure. There is a home in Calcutta where such a destitute person can spend his or her last moments of life in peace and happiness, whatever may have happened during their lifetime. There is a house of miracles in Calcutta from where such a person can make their way to their eternal home through a peaceful and beautiful death. This place is Nirmal Hriday, the old inn attached to the famous Kalighat temple.

Nirmal Hriday came about because, one day, while Mother Teresa and her sisters were still living in the house of Mr Gomez, she went with him to Mothijhil, and on the way she saw a man dying on the pavement beside the Campbell Hospital. It turned out that the reason this poor man was left to die on the side of the street was that the hospital authorities would only admit patients who could be treated for their illness. Mother Teresa and her sisters rushed to a chemist and returned with some medicines, but before they reached him, the poor man had breathed his last. They were anguished that this could be allowed to happen. 'A dog or a cat would get better treatment,' Mother Teresa said. People would not allow this to befall one of their pets. She made a complaint to the Commissioner of Police about this sad state of affairs.

Another day, she came across a bundle of clothes on the same pavement. She bent down and discovered a destitute, middle-aged woman. People were passing by right beside her, but no one had the time to stop to look at her. She was lying utterly broken down, rejected by everyone, surrounded by ants, bitten by rats and with festering wounds and pestering maggots. Touching her, Mother Teresa found that she was alive. Immediately, she lifted her up in her arms and took her to the nearby hospital. And again, the hospital staff would not admit the woman; they could not be bothered about her. But they were surprised to find that Mother Teresa would not submit to their will. She was prepared, it seemed, to move heaven and earth to have the poor woman treated in the hospital. At length, their hearts melted and they admitted the woman, but she left this world for good before very long.

Mother Teresa went once more to the Police Commissioner and requested him to grant her at least a single room some-where, where she could tend the dying destitute. The same application was submitted also to Dr Ahmet, the Health Officer of the Corporation of Calcutta. Both of them were willing to help, because they wanted to wipe out this blot on Calcutta's reputation.

Dr Ahmet took Mother Teresa to the vacant and dirty inn of Kalighat, and he asked her, 'Will this do, for the time being?'

She accepted with alacrity. Straightaway the sisters cleaned up the place and made it as suitable for human beings as they could. Mother Teresa remembered the Immaculate Heart of Mary, which attracts and accepts all the poor and the sinners with immense mercy and love. So she called that old inn by a new name – 'Nirmal Hriday', which means 'Immaculate Heart'.

It was on 15 August 1952 that she was granted this build-ing 'provisionally'. This suited the Police Commissioner and the other authorities of Calcutta very well, because the news-paper reports lamenting the state of affairs in the city began to appear less frequently. The socially minded citizens of the city also felt much relieved.

Nirmal Hriday was officially inaugurated on 22 August, the feast day of the Immaculate Heart of Mary, the Patroness of the Missionaries of Charity. In the beginning, Mother Teresa and her sisters used to find the dying destitute, who would not be admitted to hospital, on the roadside and take them in. The first person they received at Nirmal Hriday was a woman that Father Henry happened to find in the same place where the woman eaten by rats and maggots had lain. By and by, the police and the other authorities took over that duty and began to help, bringing people to them. The number of destitutes coming to Nirmal Hriday increased day by day, but God always provided the means to serve them. The people of Mothijhil came to know of Nirmal Hriday and even though they were very poor, they collected money to buy the first two cots there. Occasionally it happened that there was no cot available for a new patient. These were the times the nuns learned a new lesson of love. Without any sort of pressure from them, some of the old patients competed with each other to show their magnanimity in leaving their cots for the newcomer.

By 1998 there were two wards, one for men, the other for women, each with fifty-seven cots, and a doctor from the Corporation of Calcutta and more than twenty nurses, some of whom were nuns and some volunteers.

Nowadays, a number can be dialled to get an ambulance to take someone to a hospital and if the person is not admitted, he or she is brought to Nirmal Hriday. The record book shows that more than 69,600 dying destitutes have been admitted to date. More than half that number 'died with

God', decently and prayerfully, enjoying extraordinary peace of mind and happiness. The sisters, volunteers or co-workers washed them all, fed them, soothed them and cheered their spirits, prayed with them and for them, and thus prepared them for a happy death, which makes them fit for heaven.

Once, Mother Teresa picked up a man lying in the gutter and brought him to Nirmal Hriday. His body was full of festering wounds and nasty sores. She bathed him carefully, cleaned his sores, applied medicines and bandaged them, feeding him all the time with a dose of love and mercy. He never complained and he was not at all afraid of death. She prayed for him, and prayed with him, according to his faith. Slowly, hope of reaching heaven dawned on his face. He gave her a beautiful smile and said, 'All my life, I have lived in the street like a dirty animal; but now I am going to my eternal home like an angel,' and within three hours, he died a peaceful and beautiful death.

Mother Teresa was always very particular that the dying should receive the rituals of their faith before they die – for Hindus, a little holy water from the Ganges on their lips; for Muslims, readings from the Holy Koran; for Christians, sacramental anointing, and so on. Everyone should die peacefully and beautifully, she always maintained, in the way of his or her own faith.

Some of the patients recovered from their illness and fatigue, and were moved to another house, Nirmal Bhavan, where the nuns gave them all they needed to lead a better life here on earth. A young boy, brought to Nirmal Hriday by Mother Teresa, was cured miraculously. When he became quite healthy, the sisters wanted to shift him to the other house, but he refused to leave and remained there to help the sisters look after the patients. He went to school and college and studied well and became self-supporting in the course of time.

One day Mother Teresa happened to pay attention to one of the rubbish heaps of Calcutta. She saw a shivering, old woman lying there helplessly. Mother Teresa approached her, chasing away the dogs that were sniffing around her, and picked her up. Her body was burning with fever. She brought her to Nirmal Hriday and looked after her. She knew that the woman would not survive, so she tried to prepare her for a happy death, and that was how she came to know of the woman's greatest agony. She had only a son to depend on, but it was he who had thrown her onto the rubbish heap. She couldn't bear it. How could a mother suffer such a thing? The cruel behaviour of her only son gave the woman greater agony than the fever or the thought of her imminent death. How could she forget it? How could she forgive it? How could she stop cursing him?

Mother Teresa tried to console her and said,

God is our good Father. He created us and gave us all that we have. Yet, how many times have we committed sins against Him? Has He not forgiven us each time? Has He

66

not showered mercy on us? Hasn't He loved us? Doesn't He love us without considering any of our situations? Isn't it because of His immense love that you happened to come here? Please think it over for a minute. You too should be merciful to those who commit sins or mistakes against you. Especially, you should be kind and merciful to your son. You should forgive him. You should pray to God to bless him abundantly. You must bless him instead of cursing him.

Mother Teresa advised and compelled her again and again, and she prayed for her and with her.

Eventually, the old woman's rock-like heart began to melt. Repentance for all her sins began to fill her eyes and it made a channel down her cheeks for her tears. Lying in Mother Teresa's arms, she forgave her cruel son from the bottom of her heart. Slowly, the sign of attaining some singular peace appeared on her face, the moon of immeasurable joy and satisfaction, and it began to grow brighter and brighter. Then she looked earnestly into Mother Teresa's eyes and smiled – one of the most beautiful smiles the nun had ever seen. Then, the pearl Mother Teresa had found on the rubbish heap pronounced her sweetest last words, 'Thank you', and the next moment her soul was immersed in perfect peace and flew to eternal happiness.

Sometimes a poor creature arrived at Nirmal Hriday, whose appearance invoked nausea and revulsion. The poor soul's body would be rotten, covered with filthy sores or ulcers that emit an unbearably foul smell. When this happened in Mother Teresa's time, it was always her own special duty to attend such a patient. She would make every effort to convince these unfortunate souls that they were in her care, and that she wanted them, even if no one else in this world did. It was her prime duty to wash, clean, dress, feed and give proper medicines to these patients before all others, and slowly they would come to realize that there was indeed someone in this world who loves, cares for and looks after them as children of God, and who was ready to make any sacrifice for them. And in the end, they would become convinced that Mother Teresa was their sister and that Our Father is God in heaven, which, in turn, would pave the way for her to guide them on the right path for heaven.

She would choose the best time to instruct the patient, 'We are the children of God,' she would explain. 'Here in this world, we are just like travellers; God is Our Father and heaven is our eternal home. There we will reach one day, completing our journey in this world. There we will be free from all pain and misery and we will enjoy eternal happiness.'

When the patient was about to die, Mother Teresa would sit beside them, patting them slowly, affectionately taking one of their hands into hers and praying for and with them, and she would tell them,

You are going to die and you will reach God soon. God will be your judge to give you heaven or hell. So you must make friendship with God, your judge, by asking pardon for all the mistakes and sins you have committed in your life. He is Our Father, kind, merciful and loving. That is why you happened to come here. God will forgive you even if you were the greatest sinner, if you are sorry for your sins and if you ask pardon of Him with real repentance. Now, pray to God, saying the prayers of your religion. I shall also say the prayers that I know, so that you may reach heaven when you die.

She might now be able to witness clear signs of the dying person's love towards God, and they would pray together. Sometimes tears of repentance would start to flow. A new moon of reconciliation with God would appear on the face – an inexplicable ease and a contentment that he or she had never experienced before would begin to glow there – and the person would die beautifully with incomprehensible peace and joy.

Abhorrence, aversion, nausea and revulsion are, of course, natural in some circumstances. Once, a novice of Mother Teresa's convent came near the lavatory at Nirmal Hriday. She peeped in and ran away, almost vomiting with disgust at what she saw there. Mother Teresa did not blame this sister, who had joined the congregation with a strong determination to do and suffer anything for the sake of Jesus. Instead,

Mother Teresa rolled up her sleeves, fetched a broom and bucket, and washed and cleaned the lavatory while the young novice looked on with wonder. She came near to Mother Teresa, perhaps to ask pardon. But before she opened her mouth, Mother Teresa reassured her, 'Never mind, sister. Don't worry. It is quite natural that we feel like vomiting seeing such things, even though we are ready to do anything for Jesus. Don't worry.'

Actions speak louder than words – that was her philosophy, and what touched the heart of the novice more than Mother Teresa's words of consolation was her quick and timely action. It is the same in family life: what children remember is not the wonderful exhortation of their parents, but their edifying example. Later, this novice became Sister Superior of a Missionaries of Charity convent, but she never forgot what she had learned that day, and she was always willing to take up any dirty work that others would avoid.

It is difficult and tiring to look after the destitute people picked up from waysides and gutters, particularly when the number of those requiring close attention is high, but Mother Teresa always had many volunteers from different parts of India, England, America and Germany, who came to help in this work. They would stay for months at their own expense, in order to do selfless service at Nirmal Hriday.

I may have the gift of inspired preaching; I may have
all knowledge and understand all secrets; I may have
all the faith needed to move mountains; but if I have
no love, I am nothing .(I Corinthians 13:2)

– 8 –

Opposition and Acceptance

There were some Hindu brothers who found it impossible to tolerate Mother Teresa's deeds at Nirmal Hriday. They assembled secretly, expressed their dissent and decided on their future plan. This was how their argument went. The Kalighat is a well-known Hindu temple where there are 400 Brahmin *pujaris* (priests). It is an important place of pilgrimage, where the Holy River Ganges meets the River Hugli. Countless devotees arrive there daily, not only to name their babies, but also to cremate the bodies of their dead, and to worship Kali, the goddess of death and fertility. There is an inn attached to this temple, which is, of course, intended for the Hindu pilgrims. Well then, how can it be handed over to the Christians?

One Hindu brother went further. He claimed that at Nirmal Hriday Hindus were being converted to Christianity, and that this purpose was being whitewashed with the lie of love for fellow beings. Moreover, the argument went, those

72

who die there were often given a Christian burial. Obviously, this woman – Mother Teresa – should be thrown out, Nirmal Hriday should be destroyed, and the inn restored to Kalighat temple. Some of the young Hindus became openly hostile because they did not know the truth. One day they surrounded Nirmal Hriday and began to disturb the poor inmates and destroy the property; they shouted slogans against the sisters and threw stones at the building. At last Mother Teresa went outside to face these Hindu brothers. Jesus was with her, she said afterwards, so she told them boldly but in a humble tone, 'If you want, you can kill me; I will go to heaven. But please don't disturb the poor inmates. You won't look after them, will you? They are our fellow beings. At least allow them to die in peace.'

The Hindus saw and heard her. They were good young people, and so they did not attack the humble nun; instead, they became calm and quiet, for the time being. But they came back after a few days and lingered around the place. A party leader had given them his word that he would turn her out of Nirmal Hriday on that day and they expected to see her evicted without further delay.

Soon the Commissioner of Police and an official of the Corporation arrived to see what was going on. Poisoned by rumours, they refused any escort but roamed about the place, observing everything like suspicious, hungry vultures.

Mother Teresa was carefully removing maggots, with a pair of forceps, from the festering sores of a dying destitute, and consoling him with words of love and sympathy. 'Please say any prayer of your religion,' she told him. 'I shall say the prayer that I know. Both the prayers will please God, Our Loving Father.'

The officials watched and listened.

The sisters were going from bed to bed, serving and consoling the men and women, spreading peace and joy. Some sisters were bringing warm water to bathe patients; some were cleaning patients who had dirtied their clothes and beds with their own faeces, urine or vomit; some were washing the dirty clothes of patients, while others were putting clean ones on them; a few sisters were feeding patients with whatever food they could consume, with a spoon or with their own hands; some others were washing and dressing sores and wounds; and some were administering medicines or were rubbing the hands, legs or feet of patients who were groaning in pain; some were giving a drop of Holy Ganges water to Hindus who were about to die and were consoling and preparing them for a happy death.

The examiners saw during their hour-long survey that the sisters were serving every discarded and unwanted destitute with such a love and care as if they were announcing: You are mine and I want you, even if no one else in this world wants you. They could see that all those unwanted and discarded human beings were getting ample attention and affection that they could not get elsewhere. And what they saw changed their minds about Nirmal Hriday. They called together all the young brothers who were waiting for them outside, and then the Police Commissioner said, 'I promised your leader that I would turn that woman out of this place, and I shall. However, before I do it, you must get your mothers and sisters here, to do the work these nuns are doing. Can you do that?' When there was no answer, he continued, 'No? Then listen, in the temple we have a Devi, a goddess in stone; but here we have a Devi, a living goddess; understand?'

Hearing this, the brothers left the place one by one as the scribes and Pharisees had done when they brought to Jesus a woman caught in adultery who was to be stoned to death. When they heard Jesus say, 'Whichever one of you has committed no sin may throw the first stone at her' (John 8:7), they had no alternative but to leave the place. Similarly, the brothers who had come like hungry wolves to devour the sisters, left them alone for good.

One day, Mother Teresa found a large group of people beside the temple. They seemed afraid to approach something. She peeped in and found no poisonous snake or dangerous animal, but instead an old man, thin and sick. From the white thread he was wearing, she could make out that he was a Brahmin, and she soon realized that he was a *pujari* of Kalighat temple who had been behaving as her worst enemy with his words and deeds. Many Brahmins still could not tolerate the sight of her. The poor man was almost immersed in his own faeces and vomit. Clearly he had cholera, a contagious disease that spreads like wildfire, taking away lives within hours. Those standing around him were terrified of catching the disease, and so they were keeping their distance, doing nothing except expressing sympathy.

Mother Teresa saw in this Brahmin her beloved spouse Jesus Christ. She rushed in immediately, took him in her arms, carried him to Nirmal Hriday, washed him, dressed him in clean clothes, gave him medicine and something to drink. Slowly, his pale face began to bloom. A pleasant smile, arising from peace and satisfaction, began to linger there, along with remarkable gratitude. Then they prayed together for some time. He told her his dying wish and, accordingly, she brought some Holy Ganges water to quench his last thirst. Then, with his head on her lap, he breathed his last. A beautiful death!

Mother Teresa arranged for the cremation of his body on the bank of Holy Ganges, following the Hindu rites. Some of the *pujaris* of the temple, who had looked down on her with distrust and contempt, were deeply touched by this incident. They began to wonder whether she was the reincarnation of Kalima, because the man whom she had looked after so tenderly and lovingly in his last moments had been a great devotee of Kalima.

Another troublesome *pujari* of the Kalighat temple, who was also a great devotee of Kali and who opposed Mother Teresa tooth and nail, fell victim to consumption. Vomiting blood, after continuous coughing several times a day, the poor man was suffering badly and had become a miserable invalid. No hospital would admit him, as the possibility of his survival was very slim. Finally, his own kith and kin, as well as his fellow *pujaris*, rejected him. He was ashamed to approach Mother Teresa, as he had been so angry with her and her sisters, and he was afraid they would belittle him. However, they found him, welcomed him with open arms, brought him to Nirmal Hriday, and looked after him as if he were another Christ. They had acquired some new medicines for the treatment of tuberculosis and he began to recover. Eventually, the wild fire of his feelings of shame and anger was put out by the pouring rain of the love, care and mercy of the sisters.

Mother Teresa prayed for him daily and did whatever she could for him. 'When the strong wind of God's grace blew,' she said, 'the dark clouds of his mind also disappeared.'

Day by day, his condition improved and, after a few weeks, he was well enough to go home, taking with him the necessary medicines.

This man became a constant subject of talk among the *pujaris* of the temple, and one morning, when Mother Teresa was washing patients, he entered the ward. He came straight to her, without uttering a word, prostrated himself before her, touched her feet with his hands and laid them on his head. Then he stood and declared, 'For thirty years I have served the goddess Kalima in her temple. Now, the goddess stands before me incarnated in human form. It is my privilege to worship today the mother present to my eyes.' He would not hear Mother's denial or strong protest!

Later, she realized why some of the Hindu brothers who hated her so much did not turn her out of Nirmal Hriday by force. They had come to believe that she was the incarnation of their Kalima. This blind belief, however misguided it may have been, was a great help to her, and was responsible for the quelling of their opposition and objections. 'If we love our enemies,' Mother Teresa would reason, 'some day or other, they will turn out to be our friends.'

Although some Hindus changed their attitude towards Mother Teresa, others continued to object to her work in Nirmal Hriday on religious grounds. Some Corporation councillors sent a written complaint to the mayor:

The Kalighat Home is meant for the pilgrims of the temple of Kali Devi; yet, at the moment it is being used by Mother Teresa and other Christians to bring destitute persons to die there. This cannot be allowed on Hindu religious grounds, since they definitely defile our holy place.

Therefore they are to be evicted immediately and the place is to be restored to the Kali Temple, after performing the necessary purifying ceremony.

Mother Teresa was advised that some councillors should attend the meeting to put forward a strong argument in her favour when this item came up on the agenda. Otherwise, there was no alternative but to leave Nirmal Hriday, which, after all, had only been allotted to her provisionally.

She was not crestfallen. She put all her trust in God and in the Immaculate Heart of Mary, and she prayed day and night. When the meeting was held, the agenda was rather lengthy and when it came to the item concerning her and the sisters, only two councillors opposed Mother Teresa and her deeds at Nirmal Hriday. Their objection was duly registered and quietly forgotten. A third councillor made a suggestion: 'Let Mother Teresa continue her work at Nirmal Hriday until a suitable place is found to accommodate the dying destitute.' No one offered an alternative location, and so this resolution was passed. After that, not only were the sisters allowed to continue in Nirmal Hriday, but the Corporation also supported the Kalighat Home for the Dying with a monthly subsidy, which continued until Mother Teresa declined to accept it.

Malcolm Muggeridge approached Mother Teresa to ask if he could make a documentary film for the BBC about her work. Since she was not at all in favour of it, a persuasive letter from Cardinal Heenan was produced, to which she replied, 'If this TV programme is going to help people to love God better, then we will have it, but on one condition – that the brothers and sisters are to be included, as they do the work.' Muggeridge and the film crew agreed to this condition, so Mother Teresa said, 'Well then, let us use the occasion to do something beautiful for God.' With a smile, they began to shoot the film.

One day they came to Nirmal Hriday, but as soon as they entered, one of the crew, Ken Macmillan, said disappointedly, 'It is not possible to film here. The whole place is too dark. There are only a few windows and they are too high up on the walls. We have only a small light, and very little time. We couldn't possibly arrange for adequate light at this stage. No, we can't possibly shoot film within the short time at our disposal.'

'Why not try, at least?' Muggeridge asked.

'It would be a waste of film,' Macmillan answered, 'but if you insist . . .'

He took a few pictures in the dim light of Nirmal Hriday, and then shot a few more of patients who were sitting in full sunlight outside the home. When the film was processed, they found to their great surprise that the film shot in the dim light was much better than the one shot in the sunlight. This was something science and technology could not explain – indeed, some film that he subsequently shot in similar dim conditions turned out to be useless.

Was it a miracle? Perhaps – certainly, the BBC team were not the only people to find that photos taken inside Nirmal Hriday came out perfectly well. This was Malcolm Muggeridge's explanation: 'Nirmal Hriday is overflowing with love. This love is luminous like the haloes that artists see and make visible around the heads of saints. That is why the film shot inside Nirmal Hriday in dim light was quite clear and bright.'

Mother Teresa found that explanation very convincing, because, to her, love is light, and that light illuminates the giver as well as the receiver. Even the darkness of your heart begins to disappear, the moment you show sincere love towards your fellow beings.

It was Malcolm Muggeridge who alerted the world to Mother Teresa and her work among the poor through the BBC programme *Something Beautiful for God,* and through his book of the same title. He became an active campaigner on behalf of her work and encouraged many to do good deeds for the poor, finding God in every one of them.

God did not want to send away such a friend empty-handed.

It was natural for an educated, intelligent and well-known non-Catholic like Muggeridge to have certain doubts about the Catholic Church and the Holy Eucharist, which always gave Mother Teresa enough energy and enthusiasm to do her work. Yet, she would remind him repeatedly that the reason Jesus died on the Cross, shedding the last drop of His blood, was to save him. She wrote to him:

I am sure you will understand everything beautifully if only you would become a little child in God's hands. Your longing for God is so deep, and yet He keeps Himself away from you. He must be forcing Himself to do so, because He loves you so much as to give Jesus to die for you and for me. Christ is longing to be your food. Surrounded with the fullness of living bread, you allow yourself to starve.

The personal love Christ has for you is infinite; the small difficulty you have regarding the Church is finite. Overcome the finite with the infinite. Christ has created you because He wanted you.

When Muggeridge was in Calcutta, she told him how the Eucharist each morning kept her going. 'Without this I would falter and lose my way,' she said. 'How then could I turn aside from such spiritual nourishment?'

In fact, her humble works, requests and prayers persuaded him to reconsider his beliefs, and he once asked her, 'Tell the truth: you would like me to become a Catholic, you are praying for that, aren't you?'

She answered, 'When you possess something really good, you wish your friends to share it with you. I think that Christ is the best thing in the world, and I would like all to know Him and love Him as I do. However, faith in Christ is a gift of God, who gives it to whom He likes.'

Well, God gave Malcolm Muggeridge and his wife Kitty that precious gift and, at the age of eighty, they both embraced the Catholic faith. But though Mother Teresa was pleased about this, she never tried to make anyone a Catholic. Faith is purely the gift of God, she always maintained. In 1989, she went to visit Malcolm at his home in England and she congratulated him. Little did she know that very soon afterwards he would reach his eternal home to receive an award from God.

———

The Lord is a refuge for the oppressed, a place of safety in time of trouble. (Psalm 9:9)

– 9 –

The Gorgeous Path

In October 1950, on the Feast of the Most Holy Rosary, Father Van Exem read a Bull from Rome in the presence of Archbishop Perier, who celebrated Mass in the little chapel of Mother Teresa's congregation. Rome not only approved the congregation of the Missionaries of Charity, but also confirmed the aim for which it was established. From that day onwards, candidates came to Calcutta from different parts of India and around the world to join the congregation. Mother Teresa and her sisters sang the praises of the Lord in thanksgiving, and, in particular, she sang with the psalmist:

> I place all my trust in You my Lord;
> All my hope is in Your Mercy.

By October 1952, the congregation numbered twenty-four, and five more candidates had applied to join. The second

floor of Mr Gomez's house at Creek Lane was full, so Mother
Teresa also took the annex. By 1953, the increase in member-
ship meant that a new place was essential. However, she
found it impossible to get one, and the very thought of it
pricked her like a thorn among the sweet roses.

Just as a child clings to its mother's sari and demands that
she gives it the moon, so Mother Teresa clung to the mantle
of Our Holy Mother and she too was adamant. She recited
The Memorare 85,000 times and said that she would not give
up until she was given suitable accommodation for her children. Our Holy Mother must have persuaded Father Van
Exem and Father Henry to consider her request, because
Mother Teresa soon found that they were riding around on
their old bicycles again, searching for a house in and around
Calcutta. She maintained that Our Holy Mother became
instrumental in working a miracle for her similar to the one
that was wrought at Cana.

One day a stranger came to Creek Lane and told Mother
Teresa that if she was looking for a house, there was one at
54A Circular Road, owned by a Dr Islam, who wanted to dis-
pose of it. If she came along, the stranger said, he would
show her the house and introduce her to its owner.

Sister Agnes was standing beside her when the conversation took place, and she said, 'Mother, why don't we go and
see it now? The place is quite near and I think it is a God-
given opportunity. Shall we go?'

And so Sister Agnes and Mother Teresa followed the

stranger and reached the doctor's house. It was a magnificent building, such as they had never dreamed of.

Mother Teresa met Dr Islam and told him why they had come. He was taken aback and, without hiding his great surprise, he said that he had told no one, except his wife, that he was thinking of selling the property and going back to his homeland of Pakistan. He wondered how the sisters had come to know of it. They explained that the man accompanying them had brought them there, and they turned to the stranger, but he was nowhere to be seen.

This did not bother Dr Islam. He listened to the sisters and learned with interest who they were and what they were doing. His heart melted with pity and empathy and he declared, 'It is true that we need money in this world, but money alone will not do.'

From these words, they gathered that he would sell the building to them, if he decided to sell it to anyone. The property was very suitable for the community, with ample space for praying and for training, and would allow the sisters to live comfortably.

Father Van Exem was soon informed and he hastened immediately to the house, met Dr Islam, inspected the property, declared it a most suitable place for the Missionaries of Charity, and tried to negotiate a price.

Dr Islam appeared to be under untold pressure and tension. He said, 'Father, please come in and sit down just for a minute. Let me go to the Masjid of Moulana Ali. Let me consult with my Allah. I will not keep you waiting; soon I will return.'

When he came back, his mind was a shining silver vessel, filled with firm determination. He agreed to sell the sisters his land and building for just one and a quarter lakh (125,000 rupees). He invoked the name of his God in his next breath, saying, 'It is Allah who gave me this house, and it is Allah to whom I give back this house.'

Mother Teresa and her sisters praised and thanked the Omniscient God again and again but, although 125,000 rupees was a low price for the house, it was still a large amount of money for them and they wondered where they could get it. They led a poor life, and whatever they acquired by begging they would distribute daily among the destitute. They had no spare cash. How could they even dream of possessing such a big building? However, as Mother Teresa saw it, Our Holy Mother was there to hand over the moon into the hands of her children.

Mother Teresa approached Archbishop Perier, and after consulting with Father Van Exem and others, he was kind enough to give them a loan for the full amount, for which no interest was to be paid. Mother Teresa and her congregation were able to pay back the full amount by 1963, repaying every year whatever they could afford.

It was another miracle. It reminded Mother Teresa of the Sermon on the Mount, 'Do not fret and worry about tomorrow, your Father knows what you need. If He feeds the sparrows, will He not much more willingly give you good things, if you ask Him for them?'

In the month of February 1953, the twenty-seven sisters of the congregation moved into their new house, which the providence of God had kindly bestowed on them. It was less than a twenty-minute walk from Creek Lane and about fifteen minutes from St Teresa's parish, where they had started their first dispensary. Only God could have given them such a convenient and beautiful house and they felt they would never be able to thank Him sufficiently.

On 15 March 1953, Mother Teresa wrote to one of her friends:

> We have reached our convent at last . . .
>
> The thought that you suffer sorrows and pains pleasantly and pray to God incessantly for me, gives me immense relief as well as courage.
>
> The first ten candidates will complete their training on 12 April. They will also take their vows for one year. On that day, I shall take my final vows as well . . .

The magnificent house at 54A Circular Road, which Dr Islam offered to God, became the mother house of the congregation. It seemed incredible to the ordinary people that highly educated and energetic young women – doctors, nurses, lawyers and teachers – joined this convent of the Missionaries of Charity, where they were trained to live like the poor, with the poor and for the poor, seeing and serving Jesus in every poor person.

What the sisters are still expected to do during and after their training is quite difficult. They have to give up modern facilities and the comforts they afford. They cannot use them even when such things are offered to them, because the poor people do not have them. Not only have they themselves to be extremely poor, but they also have to be happy while they are attending to the poor, who are seriously ill and disabled, dying destitute and unwanted. The job they have to do, always with pleasure, is what others usually avoid with aversion and abhorrence. It is their task to find Jesus, not just in a manger, but also in the midst of filth such that you cannot approach without closing your nostrils. They have to find Him in the miserable invalid, abandoned by every other person in this world. They have to find Him in a mutilated and disfigured leper. They have to find Him in the tubercular patient dying on the roadside, crouching and vomiting blood. They have to find Him in the victims of AIDS, people who are avoided with fear, revulsion and hatred. They have to find Him in the unfortunate children of God who thirst for a drop of love and who suffer endlessly because of poverty, illness, oppression, depression, and all other lamentable tortures. They have to find Him in the dying destitute who crave a drop of love in their last moments. They have to find Him in the poor babies who are tormented from the moment of their birth, thrown – often by their own mothers – into the gutters or in the heaps of waste, to be left to the street dogs, the rats and the maggots. This is where the Missionaries of Charity see their beloved Jesus. They treat each one as Jesus, remembering His words in the Gospel of St Matthew, 'You did it to me.'

———

All the believers continued together in close fellowship and shared their belongings with one another . . . according to what each one needed. Day after day they met as a group . . . and they had their meals together . . . eating with glad and humble hearts, praising God, and enjoying the good will of all the people. And every day the Lord added to their group those who were being saved. (Acts 2: 44–47)

– 10 –

Secret of Success

Mother Teresa believed that suffering was the secret of success. The Missionaries of Charity have a society of those who suffer, to which many people from all over the world belong. They accept their physical and mental pain and offer it to God for the intentions of the Missionaries of Charity brothers and sisters and they pray for them. This is how it started.

One day in 1948, when the young Mother Teresa was undergoing her medical training in the Medical Mission hospital at Patna, Jacqueline De Decker, a young woman from Belgium, came in search of her. It was starting to get dark and Mother Teresa was praying in the chapel when the young woman found her. They became friends and complemented each other's lives. The young woman shared Teresa's ideals and ideas – namely to see God in the poor, and to love and serve that God wholeheartedly.

Jacqueline was a graduate of the great Catholic University of Louvain. She had specialized in sociology and had obtained a diploma in nursing and first aid. Since the age of seventeen, she had had a vocation to serve the poor in India, where she was then working in Madras.

After some time, Mother Teresa asked her, 'Jacqueline, could you please come to Calcutta with me? If you don't mind, shall we work together?'

Jacqueline agreed with pleasure and willingness, but she had first to go back to Belgium to undergo treatment. She was suffering from severe backache, and it seemed likely that she would need an operation on her spinal cord. Mother Teresa was planning to go back to Calcutta the following December to meet the poor in the slums there and to find out what she could do for them. Jacqueline promised her that she would join her in Calcutta as soon as she got relief from her back problem.

Jacqueline, a member of a rich Belgian family, never made it back to India. It was discovered that she was suffering from a severe disease of the spine and, to prevent paralysis, she had to undergo a number of operations. The surgery did not cure her and her movement was severely impaired. She had a collar round her neck, irons jacketing her body and crutches in her hands. She needed all these aids to stand up, and she was suffering immense pain.

In 1952 Mother Teresa wrote to her:

You'll be in body in Belgium, but in soul in India . . .
I need many people who suffer who would join us as I

want to have (1) a glorious society in heaven (2) the suffering society (the spiritual children) on earth and (3) the militant society, the sisters on the battlefield . . .

You must be happy, as you are chosen by the Lord who loves you so much that He gives you a part in His suffering. Be brave and cheerful and offer much that we may bring many souls to God. Once you come in touch with souls, the thirst grows daily . . .

She wrote to her again in January 1953:

My dear child Jacqueline,

I am very happy that you are willing to join the suffering members of the Missionaries of Charity – you see what I mean – you and others who will join will share in all our prayers, works and whatever we do for souls, and you do the same for us with your prayers and sufferings.

You see, the aim of our society is to satiate the thirst of Jesus on the Cross for love of souls, by working for the salvation and sanctification of the poor of the slums. Who could do this better than you and the others who suffer like you?

Your suffering and prayers will be the chalice in which we, the working members, will pour in the love of souls we gather around us. . . .

To satiate His thirst we must have a chalice. You and

the other men, women, children – old and young; poor and rich – are all welcome to make the chalice.

In reality, you can do much more while on your bed of pain than I running on my feet, but you and I together can do all things in Him who strengthens us . . .

Total surrender to God, loving trust and perfect cheerfulness – by this you will be known as a Missionary of Charity.

Everyone is welcome, but I want especially the paralyzed, the crippled, the incurables, to join . . . each one will be taken up by a sister who prays, suffers, thinks and is with her as if with a second self . . . I thank God for giving me yourself as my second self.

By now, all over the world, there are several incurables who suffer terribly with pain, each one of whom is taken up by a sister. The sister prays for that person in particular and consoles him or her. He or she in turn accepts their suffering and difficulties and offers them to God for the work of the congregation. Through letters, they share their thoughts and difficulties and treat each other as a second self, as Jacqueline and Mother Teresa did. In 1955, there were forty-eight Missionaries of Charity sisters and forty-eight patients praying together in this manner.

On 9 January 1956, Mother Teresa wrote to a friend, a member of this society, saying that 1955 had been a very fruitful year:

There are 1,114 children now studying in our schools. There are 1,416 students in our Sunday school. We have treated 48,313 patients and have helped 1,546 dying destitute.

This proves that you are not suffering in vain; you have got an equal share in our every success . . .

It is because of the suffering of these friends that we succeed in our efforts. *Thank God.*

On 26 March 1969, the Vatican recognized this group of co-workers in suffering. From that day, Jacqueline began to work as an international link between the sick, oppressed, depressed and suffering brethren. It was she who took up the most difficult job of connecting each suffering person to a particular Missionaries of Charity sister. This is how Mother Teresa expressed her message to these suffering co-workers in a letter to Jacqueline:

The Missionaries of Charity are so grateful to those who suffer for our work. We complete in each other what is wanting in Christ.

What a beautiful vocation is ours to be the carriers of Christ's love into the slums. The life of sacrifice is the chalice, or rather our vows are the chalice and your sufferings and our works are the wine – the spotless host. We stand together holding the same chalice and so with the adoring angels satiate His burning thirst for souls.

My very dear children, let us love Jesus with our whole heart and soul. Let us bring Him many souls.

Keep smiling, smiling at Jesus in your suffering – for to be a real Missionaries of Charity, you must be a cheerful victim. There is nothing special for you to do but to allow Jesus to live His life in you, accepting whatever He gives, and giving whatever He takes with a big smile.

She would tell her sisters that following Christ is inseparable from the Cross of Calvary; without our suffering, our work would just be social work, very good and helpful, but it would not be the work of Jesus Christ.

———

Your mighty deeds, O Lord, make me glad; Because of what You have done, I sing for joy. (Psalm 92:4)

– 11 –

From Candidacy to Profession

Malcolm Muggeridge once asked, 'Mother, from where do your sisters get a vocation or inspiration or inducement to join your convent and to do these sorts of services without reservation or reluctance or hesitation?'

She answered, 'From heaven, of course, from the Holy Eucharist we receive daily without fail, from the living and loving Christ; from their prayers.'

There are only some young men and women who are fortunate enough to get such an inspiration and invitation from God, but Mother Teresa considered that those who were willing to serve their fellow beings, seeing Jesus in every one of them, were the lucky ones, and she was glad to invite them with open arms to become members of the Missionaries of Charity. She promised nothing material here on earth, only peace and happiness, but she promised, without any hesitation, eternal happiness in heaven. Her guideline was always the very words of Our Lord expressed in the Gospel of St Matthew, chapter 25. And a verse that she often quoted came from the Gospel of St Luke (6:38): 'Give to others and God will give to you. Indeed, you will receive a full measure, a generous helping, poured into your hands – all that you can hold. The measure you use for others is the one that God will use for you.'

The constitution of the congregation was written originally by Mother Teresa herself, but Father Van Exem, who was both a theologian and an expert in canon law, corrected and edited it. 'Those who trust in the Lord will renew their strength. They will soar as with eagles' wings' (Isaiah 40:31).

To become a member of the Missionaries of Charity, a young person is expected to be in good health, mentally and physically; to be able to study and learn; to have a good faculty of understanding; and to have a cheerful spirit. Mother Teresa's view was that a joyful sister or brother is like sunshine in the community. Joy follows on from love; it is a need and a power. Moreover, it makes us ready to go about doing good. On one occasion Mother Teresa called back a novice who was going to Nirmal Hriday. The reason was that she found that the joy, or the pleasant nature, with which her sisters should serve the unfortunate and unhappy dying, was not fully awake in the novice's heart. She could see it on her swollen and angry face. Mother Teresa told her, 'Child, you don't seem to be well today. Please go back and take rest.' This was her reasoning:

You must always be happy to serve Jesus, for it is not you who selected Our Lord, but it is Our Lord who selected you. When such a conviction takes root in your heart, when you are prepared to follow Jesus carrying your cross, and when you listen to the sweet voice of Our Lord, all your drawbacks and defects will disappear like a thin fog in the presence of the bright sun, and joy will pervade and permeate your heart. *Thank God.*

'I thirst' is the voice of Jesus that constantly resounds in our ears. The first and foremost aim of the congregation is to try their utmost to quench this never-ending thirst for love. The way they fulfil that aim is by going out and finding those who are poor, abandoned, afflicted and thirsty and craving for a drop of love. The nuns find their beloved Jesus in these people, and look after them wholeheartedly, in accordance with the teachings of Jesus. Candidates are trained for this purpose, motivated and inculcated with the true spirit of love by their novice mistress. Mother Teresa was the first novice mistress, and it was she who undertook this training in the beginning, until she handed over the task to Sister Agnes some years later.

The training is carried out in two to three stages. Every candidate is required to visit the congregation, to get first-hand knowledge before they finally decide to join it. Fifteen days are allowed for this. Then, if they do join, they spend a year as aspirants (though in the early days of the congregation, this stage lasted only six months). During this period, the authenticity of the candidate's vocation to be a member of the congregation is examined. This is also a time for the candidate to find out whether she or he has a genuine aptitude to serve the poor, living in poverty, seeing Jesus in every individual they attend. If real dedication is lacking, the candidate may not, and should not, continue. It is also during this time that the candidate must acquire a working knowledge of English – the language of the congregation – as members come from many different places, having different mother tongues.

Candidates spend the second year training as postulants. Not only do they train to serve the poor, the sick and the dying destitute, but also they begin to learn the fundamental principles of spiritual life. After that, they will have a novitiate of two years, during which they have an intensive spiritual training in theology, Church history, scriptures and other holy books; they also acquire adequate knowledge and training in the rules of the community and in the constitution of the congregation. Apart from this, they must be fully aware of the vows they are going to take and must attain the necessary maturity through experience, realizing how each of the vows will affect them.

The vow of poverty is strict in Mother Teresa's congregation, because members must be poor themselves to be able to know and love the poor. Someone who has never been hungry will not be able to understand the hunger of the poor. Hence the Missionaries of Charity sisters must love their poverty as a mother loves her child. In fact, Mother Teresa maintained, the vow of poverty gives her sisters and brothers freedom. It frees them from selfishness. That is why they are able to laugh, and that is why they are able to keep for Jesus a clean and pure heart full of joy.

The vow of chastity requires that, of their own free will, they must offer their hearts completely to Jesus. It makes the sisters entirely united with and dedicated to Jesus and enables them to quench His thirst by seeing and serving Him, in the poorest of the poor.

By the vow of obedience they surrender themselves to do God's will in everything. There is no place for the whims and fancies or likes and dislikes of any one person. In fact, they take all other vows under obedience. As the constitution states, in order to be perfect, obedience must be supernatural in its motives, universal in its extent and entire in its execution.

Giving wholehearted free service to the poor is a vow that other congregations do not take and which binds the members of the Missionaries of Charity in a special way. This vow also means that they are to accept no money for the work they do and hence they are not to work for the rich. A holy nun at Bangalore once raised the question, when some sisters of different congregations had assembled there, whether offering free service to the poor in the way Mother Teresa did was doing more harm than good. Here is Mother Teresa's reply:

Is it not God who gave us as gifts whatever we have today? Has He done any harm to us by doing that? No. Then what is wrong in giving away as gifts what we have received as gifts? What does Our Lord Jesus Christ admonish us? If you have two shirts, give away one as a gift to someone who has no shirt.

Moreover, hasn't He given to all, in this world itself, a hundredfold of what they have given away to the poor? That is what I have experienced in my life.

When their novitiate is completed, candidates take the ceremonial first vows and begin to work as fully fledged Missionaries of Charity sisters wherever they are sent, although they continue as juniors for the next five years. During the fifth year, they undergo a special form of training known as tertianship. Each year they renew their vows and before they take their final vows at the end of the fifth year, they are sent home to their families for at least three weeks. This little holiday gives them a chance to ask themselves whether they are ready to take the final decision, whether or not they should continue on the path of serving poverty-stricken people, avoiding all worldly pleasures and modern comforts. In addition, this vacation serves to remind them that in the days ahead they will face extraordinary self-denial, total dedication, extreme poverty and hard work. Those who do not feel happy to continue the life and work of the Missionaries of Charity can stay at home. Most return to the

When Agnes, as Mother Teresa was baptized, was eight, her father died suddenly, leaving Agnes' mother to rear her and her elder brother and sister, Lazar and Aga. Here, Agnes sits on the right of her siblings.

At the age of eighteen, Agnes left everything she knew in her home country of Yugoslavia to join the Loreto Convent in Calcutta. This portrait was taken before she entered the convent.

The first twelve Missionaries of Charity whom Mother Teresa believed God had sent to help her. From the left, standing in the back row, are Sister Agnes, Sister Gertrude, Mother Teresa and Sister Dorothy.

In 1952, the sisters were granted the old and dirty inn attached to the Kalighat temple in which to treat the sick. The sisters cleaned it up and Mother Teresa named it Nirmal Hriday, the Immaculate Heart.

Mother Teresa has set up orphanages called Shishu Bhavans in sixty-one different cities, where no unwanted baby or child is ever turned away and every one is given love by the sisters.

On 10 December 1979 Mother Teresa accepted the Nobel Peace Prize in the name of the poor from all over the world. She used the opportunity to condemn abortion, about which her views were particularly strong.

Mother Teresa despised fame but at times her high profile helped her. In 1981 she wrote to the then President of the United States, Ronald Reagan, asking for his help with the famine in Ethiopia. Within hours he sent relief to the starving people there.

Working with Princess Diana helped Mother Teresa draw attention to poverty in the Bronx.

Pope John Paul II was an inspiration and guide to Mother Teresa.

Mother Teresa with the Holy Father and Sister Nirmala, Mother Teresa's right-hand woman who was elected as her successor.

Mother Teresa's death on 5 September 1997 saddened the world. The Indian government gave her a state funeral. It was a national day of mourning in India and Mass was held globally.

The simple inscription on Mother Teresa's white marble tomb is her message to us, 'As I have loved you, you too love one another.'

Mother Teresa was one of the best-loved figures of the twentieth century. Her conviction that love is what is needed for the poor has survived her.

fold, however, as, for example, Subhashini Das did, with more enthusiasm than ever to serve Jesus.

Sincere charity emerging out of pure love: that is the hallmark of the Missionaries of Charity. Mother Teresa used to tell her sisters, 'The words of Our Lord Jesus are alive even today. "Whenever you did this for one of the least important of these brothers of mine, you did it to me!"' She always believed that whenever we love the poor and serve the poor, it is Our Lord Jesus we love and serve. And whenever we suffer anything for the poor, it is for our loving Lord Jesus that we suffer.

One day, Mother Teresa answered the door to a candidate for religious life who had just completed her college studies. Mother Teresa had sent her to Nirmal Hriday at Kalighat earlier that day along with another sister, from where she returned after three hours.

'What have you been doing?' Mother Teresa asked.

The candidate replied, 'When I reached Nirmal Hriday, someone brought a wretched person, horribly stinking and with nasty and putrid sores all over his body. He was found somewhere in the gutter. With love and respect, I accepted him, looked upon him and began to tend him with great care. I washed, cleaned and carefully dressed the sores of that poor brother by applying medicine with great love and tenderness. It took three long hours. It was then that he looked at me with great relief and gave me a beautiful smile which reflects even now in the mirror of my mind! I am sure that he was the Lord Jesus himself.'

This young candidate was fully convinced of the words of Our Lord, 'I was sick, and you took care of me' (Matthew 25:36).

Most candidates who join the Missionaries of Charity come from families where they are not accustomed to such difficult work. When they came to Mother Teresa, she would take hold of their right hand in her hand, open their five fingers, and fold them one by one, saying the following five words, 'You did it to me.' The candidate and the nun would repeat those five words together and they would smile together, for they are the very words of Jesus (Matthew 25:40). They are the words that transmit immense joy to the innermost recesses of our hearts when we tend our least important brothers and sisters – the sick, the abandoned and the dying destitute. Mother Teresa would say that these five words are the five 'pills' that stimulate us to see Our Lord Jesus in these unfortunate people and to serve them with adequate love and respect. The words are a panacea that rid us of our aversion to touch, clean and serve the most unclean individuals.

During the novitiate, each candidate goes out, along with a bona fide sister, into the slums and serves the poor. They become involved in the lives of the destitute, transmitting the light of love and feeding them with the sweet honey of charity. The sisters, who have never suffered poverty, begin to experience it for the sake of Jesus and they discover that there is immense joy in suffering for Jesus. It is this joy that makes the sisters perpetually happy.

Once Malcolm Muggeridge asked Mother Teresa a very important question: 'You ask these girls, who were born and brought up in good and rich families, to live like the poorest of the poor, to devote all their time and energy and life to the service of the poor. That is asking a lot, isn't it?'

'Well, that is what they want to give,' she answered. 'They want to give everything to God. They know very well that it is to Christ the hungry, Christ the naked and Christ the homeless that they give. This conviction and this love are what makes the giving a joy. That's why you see that our sisters are very happy. They are not forced to be happy; they are naturally happy because they feel that they have found what they have been looking for.'

It is true, though, that the life is hard. The sisters get up at 4.40 in the morning, and they pray, 'Let us thank God and ask for His blessing.' They get ready as quickly as possible and come before the Holy Sacrament in the chapel at five o'clock, where they become deeply absorbed in prayer and meditation until six. Then they have Holy Mass, which is their source of strength and energy. Attending Holy Mass and receiving the Holy Eucharist in a worthy manner makes it easy for them to find Jesus in the poor they will serve. It also helps them to love and serve Jesus, enduring any kind of sacrifice or self-denial. This, in turn, makes their lives meaningful as well as joyful. In receiving Holy Communion, they hear the sweet words of Our Lord, 'Come closer to me and quench my thirst.' Here, they gather enough energy to do exactly what He wants, for there is an effective fountain that never fails to give them the encouragement, inspiration and motivation needed for their activities. That fountain is prayer, especially the beautiful prayer of St Francis of Assisi, which they recite devotedly just after Holy Mass every day:

Dear Lord,

Make us worthy to serve our fellow men throughout the world who live and die in poverty and hunger. Give them, through our hands, this day their daily bread, and by our understanding love, give peace and joy.

Lord, make me a channel of thy peace,
That where there is hatred, may I bring love;
Where there is wrong, may I bring the spirit of forgiveness;
Where there is discord, may I bring harmony;
Where there is error, may I bring truth;
Where there is doubt, may I bring faith;
Where there is despair, may I bring hope;
Where there is darkness, may I bring light;
Where there is sadness, may I bring joy.
Lord, grant that I may seek rather
To comfort than to be comforted;
To understand rather than to be understood;
To love rather than to be loved;

For it is by forgetting self that one finds;
It is by forgiving that one is forgiven;
It is by dying that one awakens to eternal life.

Mother Teresa had a way of describing how her sisters spent their days:

> As soon as we leave the chapel in the morning, each one of us transforms herself into a sort of rubber ball with which Our Lord begins to play. With jovial mind, we engage ourselves in the different jobs entrusted to us. As a rubber ball engaged in a game, each one of us, finding no place or time to rest, moves up and down hurriedly, cleaning the place, washing the clothes, cooking the food, and so on.

Breakfast is at 7.30 a.m. – a glass of water, the obligatory five chapattis, a glass of milk if American milk powder is available, or a cup of tea. It is thanks to Mother Dengel's advice that Mother Teresa always insisted that her sisters should eat five chapattis, so that they would not fall sick due to hard work and insufficient food. She would say:

> Aren't there poor beggars who can't afford even this much food? Compared to them, are we not better fed? Do the poor have any washing machine to wash their clothes? No. That is why we refused with thanks an offer to donate to us washing machines. The clothes we wear on the

previous day we wash in the morning. We have no servants in any of our institutions; we are our own servants.

Breakfast takes fifteen minutes, and then each sister goes to her place of work – Nirmal Hriday, Premdan, the slum areas, Shishu Bhavan, leprosy relief centres, TB hospitals, clinics, dispensaries, the homes of the destitute, orphanages, or wherever her duty takes her. According to their rules, they always go in twos. This is not because they are afraid of anyone – for not a single sister of the congregation has ever been a victim of any heinous crime anywhere in the world, and Indians, in particular, are respectable people who know how to respect holy persons.

The sisters travel like poor people, often on foot. If they have to travel by any vehicle, they usually choose the cheapest mode of transport, and on the journey they keep the company of Jesus and Mary, saying prayers or the Rosary. They offer all their actions to God, by which they convert them into sweet prayers.

When it is time for their noon meal, the sisters return to the house. They are reminded of Mother Dengel's advice that they should eat enough to continue their work without falling prey to illness. Similarly, following another piece of advice from Mother Dengel, they divide the day in two and rest for half an hour after lunch. After this siesta, they spend some time in spiritual reading. Then they have a cup of tea and proceed to do their work energetically.

Sometimes sisters are entrusted with different jobs, since this helps to renew their energy. All are supposed to return to the convent by six in the evening, when they have adoration and Rosary in the chapel before the Holy Sacrament until 7.00 p.m. Then they have their simple supper – rice, dal and some vegetables – like the poor people eat certainly, but enough to survive. Meanwhile, they have spiritual reading for some time. When the Superior says '*Laudatur Jesum Christum*', everyone says 'Amen' and the silence is broken. The voice of joy is audible, though the day's experience which they narrate is nothing out of the ordinary.

After supper, they have time for recreation and for mending. They keep their mending things – needles, darning thread, a razor blade, buttons and so forth – in a cigarette tin. At 9.45 p.m. they assemble again in the chapel for silent prayer, examination of conscience and community prayer, and at 10 p.m. they go to bed, offering themselves into the hands of God the Father, and they usually fall quickly into a deep sleep.

This is more or less the pattern of the day in all the Missionaries of Charity convents, but, of course, it may vary a little from place to place.

When the others are asleep, Mother Teresa would take the opportunity to keep up with her correspondence, though occasionally she would be so tired herself, she would put her head down on the table for a little while, and a sound sleep would cover her with its soft blanket. Even so, she always woke up at 4.40 a.m. for the start of the new day.

On Thursdays, some of the sisters take leave from their regular work. That is a day meant for doing things for oneself, like mending torn clothes, washing and cleaning. Some sisters also find special time on Thursdays for religious studies and meditation. Once a year, the sisters are allowed to go on an excursion. On that day, they entrust their duties to the novices, who gain experience and self-confidence from this opportunity.

The sisters do not have anything to call their own except a rosary, a crucifix, a plate and three saris – two for daily wear and a third one for special occasions. At the same time, they remember that their poorest brothers and sisters do not own even this much. Only in the visitors' room do they have a fan, and also for the benefit of others they have a telephone connection. People used to say that it was a miracle that the telephone in the mother house in Calcutta never broke down.

As it is mentioned in the constitution, the life of the sisters is based on ideals of love, total surrender, loving trust and cheerfulness. They must be able to radiate the joy of Christ and should express it in their actions. They want to make the people feel that they are loved. They accept everything with cheerfulness, as that is the most befitting manner to express gratitude towards God and men.

Dear friends, let us love one another, because love comes from God. Whoever loves is a child of God and knows God. (I John 4:7)

– 12 –

Miraculous Experiences

Mother Teresa once explained how she was drawn to work with babies and children:

> About 2,000 years ago, at midnight in December, the piercing cry of a newborn babe arose from a manger at Bethlehem. It was the cry of the Infant Jesus, the Redeemer of the world. Whenever the piercing cry of an unwanted and abandoned babe reaches my ears, it appears to me as the very same crying of the Infant Jesus. Can I ever ignore the cry of my Jesus?
>
> That is why a small Nazareth or Nirmal Shishu Bhavan came into being near our mother house on 23 September 1955, and why Shishu Bhavans were established in sixty-one different cities. Every child that is thrown away by nurses or mothers, married or unmarried, in hospital buckets, gutters, canals, waysides, dustbins, drains or heaps of rubbish, is a precious jewel

created by God Almighty. Sometimes, parents don't want a child that is born prematurely, crippled, physically or mentally handicapped or is a victim of AIDS, but we want it and we look after them all as if each of them were the Infant Jesus.

We are unable to impart the same sacred and real love as a mother who carried the child in her womb, yet we love every child. No child will ever be refused in our Shishu Bhavan, even if it means that two or three have to share the same cot or they have to be coaxed into life in a box heated by a light bulb. Every child is a magnificent and miraculous present given to us by God. Even the child that is going to die within a few moments needs to be loved and consoled, for it has the ability to recognize human love.

The Shishu Bhavan, which the sisters started in Calcutta, was, for them, a replica of Nazareth, where Jesus was brought up. Every day Mother Teresa went there, she would take each child to her bosom, and give it her love and affection, as if that child were the same Infant Jesus. Whenever she was afraid that the light of life in a child was going to be extinguished, she quickly wrapped the babe in flannel and entrusted it to a sister, instructing her to give it special attention, to administer to it with all the love and care she could muster. Once, she entrusted a dying child to a sister for her special care. The child enjoyed her love and the warmth of her bosom, her lullaby and sweet voice. But that evening the child breathed its last, like a faded flower. 'It is my ambition,' Mother Teresa said then, 'that not even a single child should die without enjoying love.'

One day the feeble cry of an infant was heard from the very altar of the Sacred Heart Church in Calcutta. The sacristan rushed to the place and found an abandoned baby. He brought some milk, and as soon as it was fed, the babe slipped into a sound sleep. Meanwhile, the police were informed and they entrusted the baby boy to Mother Teresa. He was brought up in the love and affection of Shishu Bhavan, and before long, was adopted by a good family and is now doing very well.

Sometimes people leave their children on the sisters' doorstep, or unmarried mothers bring their unwanted children to them. Some babies end up in Shishu Bhavan because someone phones the sisters to tell them about them, and most of these infants are physically or mentally disabled. At other times, the sisters find abandoned children in the streets, or the police bring them to the sisters. The sisters have nothing, yet they are able to feed and to look after every child who happens to reach Shishu Bhavan. 'Is it not a big miracle?' Mother Teresa would ask with a smile.

When she accepted the Nobel peace prize in Oslo on 10 December 1979, she told the distinguished guests assembled there what she felt about abortion:

The greatest destroyer of peace today is abortion because it is a direct war, a direct killing, a direct murder by the mother herself.

Many people are very, very concerned with the children of India, with the children of Africa, where quite a number die, maybe of malnutrition, of hunger and so on; but in the developed world, millions are dying by the will of the mother.

Similarly, at the celebrations for the fortieth anniversary of the United Nations, when a documentary film about her work was being screened, she was asked to address the guests who had assembled there from many different countries. Mother Teresa told them:

We are afraid of a new disease called AIDS, but we are not afraid of killing brutally an innocent child, are we? The greatest enemy of world peace today is nothing but abortion.

'Why are we not worried about such heinous deeds?' Mother Teresa would ask, for she believed that there is nothing more heinous in this world than the willingness of a mother to kill her own child in her own womb by crushing or cutting it into pieces. She even went so far as to say that parents who procure an abortion, and all those who render any help for abortion, deserved capital punishment. They will be asked to give account to the Almighty here on earth or in the other world, she maintained, and for this reason she would plead with distressed parents not to kill a baby they did not want, but instead to give it to her and her sisters, so that it would have a chance to grow up happily in one of their Shishu Bhavans.

In addition to looking after unwanted or abandoned babies, Mother Teresa would also welcome into her care unmarried mothers who were in despair – sometimes even driven to attempt suicide. The sisters give shelter to these women until their babies are born, and after that, they can leave the baby with the sisters and go back to their lives. Then the sisters have the double satisfaction of saving two lives.

Indira Gandhi was a great friend of Mother Teresa's, but Mother fiercely opposed her policy of vasectomy and other surgical sterilization. She told her frankly what she believed – that she would lose the blessing of God for this sort of programme. She thought that perhaps Mrs Gandhi was beginning to listen to her. When she was defeated in a parliamentary election, in spite of their differences on this issue, Mother Teresa still went to console her friend.

There is nothing spectacular in any of the sisters' institutions, but beautiful and colourful things adorn all the Shishu Bhavans – things that are attractive to children, the toys the sisters would like to present to the Infant Jesus. These things are just a small part of their great desire to provide the children with whatever they need. There is always room to accept one more child in every Shishu Bhavan. The Almighty who looks after the birds of the sky and the lilies of the field carefully gives the sisters whatever is needed to protect and nurture these babies too.

One day when 150 children were in the Shishu Bhavan in Calcutta, all precious jewels, the sisters found to their great dismay that there was not a single drop of milk left to feed them. What could they do? The children cried, but who was there to hear the cry of the sisters? It was the God of Mercy who listened to their cry. All at once, there arose in the mind of a Hindu brother the voice of conscience that sounded like an order he could not disobey. 'Take all the milk you possess, rush to the Shishu Bhavan in Calcutta immediately, and give it to Mother Teresa.' Every heartbeat of that brother was a resonance of that order, and he told Mother Teresa that the orders ceased only when he had met her. She opened the can he brought to her, measured the milk, and found that it was the exact measure of milk they needed for the children that day.

Every child who reaches a Shishu Bhavan has a pathetic story to tell, stories that might have ended in tragedy, but it is the wish of the sisters to give every story a happy ending. Good people from India and abroad come to the Shishu Bhavans almost daily, motivated by an intense desire to adopt a child. Magnanimous people from different countries – France, Canada, Switzerland, among others – adopt children who might not otherwise be adopted because they are seriously ill or have a physical or mental disability. Such people do not look for external attractiveness or beauty when adopting a child. Couples who have children or who expect to have children of their own can also adopt a child from the Shishu Bhavans. However, the sisters always ensure that the future of such children is bright and safe.

Not every child is adopted, however, and the older boys, who can no longer be kept in Shishu Bhavan, are moved to Bala Bhavan, which is run by the Missionaries of Charity brothers. There, they are given a proper education, trained for work and helped to find a job. Sponsors are also found for the children who are not adopted, and thousands manage to complete their studies with the help of generous sponsors from India and abroad.

Even if the adoptive parents live in a foreign country (in this respect, free passes granted by the airlines have helped greatly), the sisters visit the children where they are being brought up and they enquire about them until they are capable of standing on their own two feet. For example, Mother Teresa herself went to Geneva to visit children who had been adopted there from Shishu Bhavan. The first child on her list was Bablu, who had been adopted by the Miller family. Bablu's father had been a poor porter at Siliguri railway station, who had become ill with tuberculosis through hard work and poor food. He did not live long, and left behind his seven-year-old son. The poor boy was found by the sisters, bedridden and unable even to sit up. They treated and looked after Bablu for two years, until Joe Miller and his family adopted him. They brought him up as their own child, educated him, and provided him with whatever they could afford.

Bablu is a Swiss citizen today. He works as a cook in a dining hall run by an international agency. He is now a self-reliant and healthy young man, and a member of a football team. Mother Teresa was delighted at the mere sight of him, and indeed most of the children adopted in India and abroad get a good position in life when they grow up.

There is no question of rejecting or neglecting any child that happens to reach any of the Shishu Bhavans. By 1997, there had been 14,000 children in the Shishu Bhavan of Calcutta alone. More than 5,000 of this number were adopted by people from different countries, where they now live happily, and others were transferred to various Bala Bhavans, where they were educated and trained in such a way that they could become independent and find suitable work. In 2001 there were 430 children in the Shishu Bhavan in Calcutta. Each child is well looked after and well fed by God Almighty.

From an early age, Mother Teresa had been brought up to have a great devotion to Our Lady, and she always claimed that Our Holy Mother assisted her throughout her life. She made it a habit to carry a few medals of Our Lady wherever she went, which she would give to people she met.

Sometimes on her travels, she would reach a certain place, and would take some of these medals and bury them in the sand. At other times, she scattered them here and there, saying a few Hail Marys as she did so. The sisters never asked her why she did it, but this was the reason: when her conscience dictated to her that it was essential to erect a home for the destitute, a Shishu Bhavan, or some other Missionaries of Charity institution at a certain place, she studied the environment as far as possible to choose a location. Spontaneously, her right hand would search in her bag for the medals and she would bury or scatter them in a few places, placing all her trust in Our Holy Mother.

Then she would wait, like a gardener who had sown some precious seeds, as she put it herself, to see how and when they would begin to sprout, all the while, humbly supplying, relentlessly and regularly, the moisture and warmth that was needed for growth. Eventually a property, where she had deposited the medals of Our Holy Mother, would become a part and parcel of the work of the Missionaries of Charity. Soon one of its institutions would spring up there, giving shelter to many, like a well-grown fruit tree.

Some people might think this is a mere superstition, but to Mother Teresa it was simply a matter of faith. She would say:

Let me proclaim as loud as I can that it is due to the miraculous intercession of Our Holy Mother that a leprosy centre or a mental asylum, or a house for the handicapped, or a Shishu Bhavan came into existence at certain places. Nothing is impossible, the moment Our Holy Mother intercedes for us. Anyone who takes shelter at the feet of Our Holy Mother at the time of their necessity will be able to join me and St Bernard to proclaim that Our Lady will never reject or refuse any of our earnest requests.

Mother Teresa was returning one day to Calcutta from Rome, carrying some medicines for the poor. The aeroplane landed at Delhi airport fifteen minutes late. It was 7.30 in the evening when she reached the terminal and her flight to Calcutta was due to take off at 8 o'clock. She met a friend and told him that she had medicine in one of her boxes for a boy whose life was sinking in the Shishu Bhavan in Calcutta, medicine that might save him, but that her luggage had not yet been unloaded from the plane. She asked him to help to get her and her boxes onto the plane for Calcutta. Her friend's gestures made it clear that this was impossible.

The terminal building was full of people wanting to meet Mother Teresa and get her autograph, but the only person she was concerned about was the boy in Calcutta whose life was in danger, and whom she feared she would not reach in time with the medicine. She told her story to the people around her, and the word spread around the airport. Our Holy Mother, who always helped Mother Teresa in any urgent need, was there alive in her mind, so Mother Teresa took out her rosary beads and started to say the Rosary. By the time she had finished the first decade, all the workers in the airport, from the porter to the senior officer, were alert and willing to render her all possible help.

The plane for Calcutta was almost ready to take off. It was already moving towards the runway, and still she was waiting for her luggage. Suddenly, the captain received a message from the control tower, and immediately the plane came to a halt. Air traffic control had told the captain that there would be a short delay in takeoff. Within seconds, the door of the aeroplane was opened again, and Mother Teresa's six boxes were placed inside. By now, she had recited all five decades of the Rosary, and someone had driven her to the plane. As soon as she boarded, it took off for Calcutta. This was one of several miracles that Our Lady worked for Mother Teresa, but, of course, there were also lots of helpful people involved in solving her problem, and she was grateful to all of them for their co-operation.

———

Let the children come to me and do not stop them because the kingdom of God belongs to such as these . . . Whoever does not receive the kingdom of God like a child will never enter it. (Luke 18:16–17)

– 13 –

Tents of Miracles

Two thousand years ago, when Christ was moving around Galilee doing good to all, lepers had no place in society. They were outcasts. That is why one day a leper approached Jesus stealthily and cried, 'Lord, you can make me clean if you want to', and Our Lord immediately extended His helping hand, touched him and said, 'I do want to. Be clean.' At once the disease left the man and he was clean. But if he wanted to mingle with society, he had to get a certificate from the priest which stated that he was cured. So Jesus told him, 'Go straight to the priest and let him examine you; then in order to prove to everyone that you are cured, offer the sacrifice that Moses ordered.' (Mark 1:40–44)

Mother Teresa always believed that, as Jesus had such sympathy for lepers, we too must have genuine sympathy for them. Like Jesus, we too must do for that individual whatever we can. She had a story about Francis of Assisi and a leper:

St Francis of Assisi once met a miserable leper who had a deformed nose and swollen eyes and pus oozing from his lips and ears, and disfigured hands and feet. The poor leper stretched his fingerless arms out to St Francis and begged for alms.

St Francis had nothing to give that beggar except his heart filled with the warmth of love. To share that love with him, St Francis smiled, accepted him with open arms and embraced him, impressing his great love on him with a sweet kiss.

The leper wanted to return it in the same coin. He clutched Francis close to his chest, hugged him hard, and kissed him back, ignoring the fact that his swollen lips were oozing pus and blood. At the next moment, the entire place was filled with sweet fragrance and with heavenly light. And where was the leper? He was not to be seen!

St Francis of Assisi understood and he cried out to his disciples, 'That was not a leper, but our loving Jesus Christ Himself!'

In Mother Teresa's time in India, leprosy was a major problem, and this is another of her stories:

Once a leper happened to arrive at the gate of Sabarmathi Ashram of Gandhiji [this is the affectionate name by which Mahatma Gandhi was known to Indians], but not a single inmate of the Ashram would allow him in. Gandhiji came to know of it. He came out immediately and welcomed the leper with great pleasure and told his companions, 'God wants to test me. So, He has appeared today in front of me as a leper.'

On one occasion, five poor lepers approached Mother Teresa. They had lost their jobs when they became victims of the disease, and soon they were being treated like dogs by their own families and were thrown out of their homes. They found no place of shelter anywhere. They had no other alternative but to leave their homeland, migrating to a faraway place, and living there as unknown beggars. When they met Mother Teresa and shared their untold misery and mental agony with her, it affected her heart deeply. She found herself burning in their fire of agony. She found no way of escape, unless she discovered some way out for them.

And so Mother Teresa could not ignore the terrible plight of lepers. She went into their midst with immense pleasure, bringing proper treatment and service, food, clothing and shelter, and above all she brought the nectar of love. Her delight had no bounds, because she found Jesus in each one of them, as St Francis of Assisi had done. Mother Teresa herself tended lepers, towards whom many might feel aversion and abhorrence, and every time she did so, she claimed that she too experienced inexpressible joy. She recommended to the people around her to see Jesus in the lepers they met; that way, they too would experience that same ecstasy.

The big problem with leprosy is people's fear and prejudice, she would explain. Even highly qualified people lose their jobs if they are found to have this disease. Lepers are ostracized in their own home and homeland, and are shunned by their own families. Even a highly educated person, if he or she becomes a leper, has to face disgrace, insult, ignominy, excommunication, banishment, anonymity, poverty and starvation.

Mother Teresa campaigned hard to educate people about leprosy, which can be fully cured if proper treatment is given from the very beginning. It is true that people do have to be cautious about leprosy that is not being treated, as it can flare up. But, just as the damage caused by fire can be prevented by stamping out the fire early, so leprosy will subside if it is treated in time. The disease spreads because of poverty, which leads to dirty and unhealthy conditions. It was rampant in Europe in the twelfth century, but by the nineteenth century it had been eradicated from the continent. Smallpox has been eradicated for good from India, and the same thing can be done for leprosy if people really want to make it happen.

There are millions of lepers in India today, most of whom suffer from non-infectious forms of the disease, but even infectious patients cease to be contagious after some weeks' treatment with modern drugs under the regimens advocated by the World Health Organization. It is important to consult a competent doctor as soon as the symptoms emerge. The longer patients ignore their condition, or try to hide it, the more harmful it will turn out to be. If people with leprosy neglect to see a doctor, the illness will spread to the nervous system, and they will start to lose sensation in their limbs, with the result that they will not notice pain. Wounds and ulcers can easily occur, and eventually the nose and ears will be disfigured and certain parts of the body will be shrivelled and distorted. Eyelashes will fall out and, finally, limbs will be lost. But if treatment is sought in time, all these problems can be avoided.

Lepers are our brothers and sisters, and since, in these modern times, we have the expertise to operate and to treat and cure them, Mother Teresa reasoned that we are clearly obliged to use it, for they have the right to lead a decent life like the rest of us. That should be obvious, but when the city of Calcutta was expanding, what did the government – of the people, for the people and by the people – do but close down the leprosy hospital at Gobra. Dr B. C. Roy was then Chief Minister of Bengal. A great friend of Mother Teresa's, she could approach him at any time without an appointment because he knew that she would never come to him for any of her personal needs. But even he denied her earnest request to save the Gobra Hospital. He offered another place to her and her sisters for a hospital, but she could not accept it, since it did not have a supply of clean water.

Mother Teresa felt she had no choice but to find a more

suitable location to open a clinic for the Gobra lepers. However, a local councillor raised the red flag of his power and blocked her attempts. When she arrived with her sisters at Mothijhil, where they proposed to build their rehabilitation centre, this councillor, along with the villagers, threw stones at her. Mother Teresa understood that it was ignorance, fear and suspicion of leprosy that was the cause of their actions, and so she did not blame anyone. Instead, she ran back to their van, consoling the sisters and saying, 'It seems that God does not want us to start a leper clinic here. Let us pray to know what His will is.'

Mother Teresa had to come up with another way of helping those poor lepers, and so the sisters prayed for two months to know the will of God. During this time, Philips Electric Light Company made a donation of 10,000 rupees. Also, an ambulance was sent to the sisters from the United States, which became the first of Mother Teresa's mobile clinics for lepers. Archbishop Perier inaugurated it in September 1957. Now, not only the lepers of any particular area, but from all over Calcutta could begin to get care and attention and proper medicines. From that time onwards, Mother Teresa understood the Psalm: 'If the Lord does not build the house, the work of the builders is useless' (Psalm 127:1).

Meanwhile, Jesus, who said, 'I am with you, don't be afraid of anything', wanted to help the sisters in their humble endeavours, and so He inspired a great man to render them all possible help. Dr Sen, a specialist in leprosy treatment at the Carmichael Hospital, had retired from his official post and now he offered his services free of charge to Mother Teresa's leprosy work for as long as he was able, not only treating lepers himself, but also training the brothers and sisters to treat them, using modern medicines and techniques. Dr Chadha is another doctor whose free service has saved lepers, especially in Delhi.

Using the mobile clinic, Mother Teresa and her co-workers were able to bring the appropriate drugs to those suffering from leprosy, as well as medicines for other ailments, free milk, rice, clothes and blankets. Hundreds of lepers assemble when the mobile clinic arrives each week, and they receive medicines, food packets, clothing and the fare for their journey. Mother Teresa had reason, in the end, to be grateful to that councillor who objected to her centre at Mothijhil. 'The Omniscient God knows how to reap goodness even from evil,' she claimed.

Medical advances meant that patients could be treated in their own homes, and of course it is a great blessing for the patients to be able to remain with their families, their essential source of love, and in employment, the mainspring of their dignity. Before long, effective medicines arrived from countries like England and America, and the Missionaries of Charity today can completely cure a leper within two years of treatment.

Mother Teresa felt that she had also succeeded, to some extent, in changing the negative and fearful attitudes to leprosy. However, she would add, 'God has not called me to be successful but to be faithful.' She wanted the lepers, who had been cured, to be trained so that they could take up jobs. Instead of begging, she wanted them to be able to lead a decent life, like any other responsible citizen of India. She wanted to restore the dignity and confidence of the patients whose sense of identity had been undermined by constant fear. She wanted to change the idea 'once a leper, always a leper'. And she provided the lepers with all necessary help – food, clothing, shelter, jobs and guidance towards self-sufficiency. She managed, with the help of the Lord, to provide suitable centres for the rehabilitation of those who are fully recovered from the disease and peaceful shelters for dying lepers.

Another councillor also fought to defeat Mother Teresa's plan for serving and uplifting the miserable lepers of Calcutta. One day, he was thrown out of his own house because his family discovered that he too was a victim of leprosy. Only then did he realize the miserable plight and agony of a leper. Thus the petitioner became the accused; the wild wolf became a tamed lamb. This poor lamb, however, did not find any fold to rest its head at night, but was forced to wander from place to place until the sisters found him and gave him shelter. He was astonished at the sincere love, service and treatment they lavished on him. He could not understand how he, their number one enemy, could obtain so much pardon, forgiveness and love. Later he learned that Our Lord Jesus forgave even those who crucified Him. With the help of the Lord, the sisters' continuous and timely treatment cured him of his disease, and in later years he became one of the leading people helping in the care of lepers, even working alongside Mother Teresa herself as her right-hand man in running a leprosy relief centre.

When a wealthy businessman remarked to Mother Teresa, 'I would not touch a leper for a thousand pounds', she replied with a smile, 'Neither would I, but I would willingly tend him for the love of God.' This incident prompted her to start Leprosy Day to raise funds to help lepers. 'Touch a leper with your compassion' was the motto inscribed on the collection boxes. When the boxes were opened, it was clear that the citizens of Calcutta had responded with great generosity, and Mother Teresa was very pleased to find that, over time and partly as a result of her campaigning, many people had abandoned their fear and suspicion.

Mother Teresa told the story of how she once approached a woman in one of the sisters' homes for the destitute. Lying curled up like a question mark, the woman was clearly in mental pain, and Mother Teresa tried to console her. It turned out that she was the former matron of a renowned private school in Calcutta, who had become a victim of leprosy. She did not disclose her situation to anyone, nor did she try to get treatment for it. She kept it secret for a long time, but eventually her nervous system was affected, loss of limbs resulted and the hidden truth came to light. Then she became a great burden even to her own children. Her youngest son, who used to love her very much, brought her to the sisters. The eldest son did not bother about her at all. Not even once did he think of coming to see his sick mother! With tears in her eyes, that poor woman asked, 'Mother, my beloved youngest son visited me last Christmas. Will he come again next Christmas?'

Only love, mercy and kindness can change the mentality of the poor leper who feels so outcast and unloved, Mother Teresa believed, and charitable deeds can convince the leper that his or her illness is not a punishment sent by God.

'Let us mould our minds and our deeds,' Mother Teresa used to say, 'in such a way as to hear, on the last day of judgment, the sweet words of Our Lord, "Come and possess the kingdom which has been prepared for you ever since the creation of the world because . . . I was sick and you took care of me . . ." *Thank God.*'

For indeed, leprosy is not a punishment, she used to argue, but a precious gift from God that is meant to enable us to love and serve those affected by it. It is our duty to convince these poor people that there is someone in this world who wants them and loves them and that a leper's life is worth living. It is for this that the sisters strive in their leprosy centres, and in all their activities and sincere efforts, God's grace incessantly helping them, like oxygen in the air they breathe. This help has brought miracles in each centre, for its rise, growth and development.

Far from the city of Calcutta, near the town of Asansol,

there is a peaceful place that is marked by the beauty of a village and conveniences of a small town. It is none other than the leprosy relief centre named Shanthi (peace) Nagar (town), which was established in 1957. The thirty-four acres of land at Shanthi Nagar were given to Mother Teresa for a rent of just one rupee a year for thirty years. The miracle-worker was Mr Jyothi Basu, the Chief Minister of West Bengal, the well-known Communist leader and friend of Mother Teresa's who never refused any of her requests.

Before it was given to the sisters, Shanthi Nagar was a jungle, but Sister Albert and Sister Francis Xavier succeeded, within a short time, in converting it into a place suitable for dwelling as well as for cultivation. It has been transformed into a beautiful garden where Mother Teresa's dreams of helping her dear lepers bear fruit.

It was Mother Teresa's dream to have a place for lepers where they could live and die with dignity, where they could work gainfully and lead constructive lives, and Shanthi Nagar is now not only a renowned leprosy relief centre, where modern technology and medicines are available to cure lepers, but also a place where lepers can live like decent and dignified citizens. The moment patients are able to work, they are given proper training and regular remuneration. They are helped to lead a family life of peace and happiness.

In 1964, the Holy Father Pope Paul VI came to Bombay to inaugurate the Eucharistic Congress, and he took the opportunity to visit Nirmal Hriday, driven in a white

Lincoln, which had been donated by America. The Holy Father was so pleased with the sisters' work that he presented the car to Mother Teresa, but of course she preferred to walk, and had no personal use for the vehicle. Instead, she raffled it, raising hundreds of thousands of rupees which were used to fund the building of family cottages at Shanthi Nagar. It was the rehabilitated lepers themselves who made the bricks and built the cottages in the style of their own villages.

The children of the lepers of Shanthi Nagar are also free from the fear of leprosy. They can study, grow and acquire positions in life like any other citizen in India. They can assemble and play and never feel that they are separate from the rest of the society. On the contrary, they understand that they too are the children of the same God the Father and that they too will become people who will contribute to society.

It is the cured and trained lepers also who are responsible for the flower and fruit gardens of Shanthi Nagar and they produce not only sufficient vegetables but also enough rice and wheat to meet their needs each year. They constructed the fish ponds, which produce sufficient fish to supply the needs of the community. They also have a dairy farm, keep poultry and pursue other cottage industries, which make them self-sufficient in every respect. Nothing is allowed to go to waste. All waste materials are collected for compost, and gas is produced from cow dung. 'Above all,' Mother Teresa never tired of saying, 'God blesses and rewards abundantly all the works done by the distorted and shrivelled hands and feet of the lepers. Anyone who visits Shanthi Nagar will wonder at the marvellous works of Our Lord!'

Several non-Christian doctors render selfless service to the hundreds of inhabitants of Shanthi Nagar. Two or three of them travel to the centre from Asansol or Dhanbad at least once a fortnight and perform the surgery that rectifies the deformity of the lepers. By 1998, nearly 10,500 people had undergone successful operations, 5,650 pairs of special shoes had been made, forty-five persons had been given equipment to help them to speak, 16,205 had been admitted to the hospital and 44,500 had been treated in the out-patient clinic. In addition, 15,500 other patients were also treated there. By that year, 750 children had been admitted to the Shishu Bhavan. Nearly 1,000 persons are given rations every month and 500 are given daily food. Moreover, forty students are studying in the schools nearby. Currently, there are eighty fully cured lepers in Shanthi Nagar, all employed in either the hospital or in the fields, with a sense of utter dedication and self-respect.

Before the hospital at Gobra was closed down, the sisters used to examine lepers in front of the Entally convent every Wednesday. They would give the patients medicines, vitamin tablets and packets of food. For this reason, poor patients used to arrive from as far away as Titlagarh, sometimes without paying the bus or train fare. They carried along with them their small children and suffered untold miseries to get this help. It was their miserable plight that made Mother Teresa decide she should visit Titlagarh.

The poor lepers used to assemble under a big tree in Titlagarh, waiting for the mobile clinic van. The very sight of that van used to fill their hearts with joy and satisfaction, as if they had found some great treasure. Day by day, their number increased, and very soon Mother Teresa came to realize that a clinic needed to be set up. There was immediate opposition, but she was fond of the saying that 'necessity is the mother of invention', and so she set up a temporary shed beside the railway line. Within a few months, she had started a clinic, which she entrusted to a handful of Missionaries of Charity sisters. The number of patients attending the clinic increased so much that three or four sisters could not manage them. Moreover, the area around the clinic was marshy, unhealthy and full of poisonous snakes. Clean drinking water was not available there, and most of the people had not so much as a small hut to sleep in at night. Above all, there was continuous trouble from local criminals and troublemakers. Mother Teresa decided that it would be a better idea to put some of the Missionaries of Charity brothers in charge of the clinic, and they did wonders there within a short time.

Meanwhile, she had informed the municipal authorities what was going on at Titlagarh. She had also sent them applications and reminders, one after another. At last, the miracle happened. The authorities blessed the work and, in October 1960, they leased the sisters the entire narrow piece of land between the railway line and the Titlagarh municipal sewage pumping station, ignoring all opposition. But that was not the only miracle at Titlagarh. Brother Christu Das and Brother Mariya Das tried their level best to improve the lives of the poor lepers, but they continued to be subject to attack by criminals. Abusive words, quarrels and stones from these *goondas* did not deter the brothers from their work. They suffered everything bravely, forgave their enemies wholeheartedly and loved them all sincerely. Above all, they prayed for those who were doing great harm to them day and night. Then the second miracle happened. The darkness of enmity, hostility and violence started to disappear in the light of their tolerance, love and sincere service, and it became possible for the brothers to build houses for the lepers, so that now those who slept on the roadside could have a roof over their heads.

The progress that the sisters and brothers made within a few months was much beyond their expectations. The railway authorities noticed it and took pity on the lepers and those who were working to help them. As a result, yet another miracle occurred: all the land extending about a mile from the railway station at Titlagarh to Kurda station was transformed into a beautiful rehabilitation centre. Today, any visitor can see the office of the Gandhiji Prem Nivas, wards for male and female patients, the wonderful workshop where the cured lepers earn their livelihood decently by doing various jobs, an agricultural field and a refectory. Is it not a miracle that all these things came into being unexpectedly within a very short time?

———

Lord, if you want to, you can make me clean.
(Matthew 8:2)

– 14 –

The Brothers of the
Missionaries of Charity

It was on 25 March 1963, with the blessing of the archbishop, that the congregation of Missionaries of Charity brothers was inaugurated. The brothers carry out the same kind of work as the sisters, and the male patients, in particular, like to be attended by the brothers.

On that same day another important event took place. A young Australian named Ian Travers-Ball became a Jesuit priest. Mother Teresa was not to know at the time, but this young priest had been selected by God Almighty to work along with her to love and serve India's poor. In 1964, while he was doing his tertianship at Sitagarah in Hazaribagh, he obtained permission from his superiors to work for a month amongst the poor, which is how he happened to become involved with the Missionaries of Charity brothers. He was so much attracted to their work that he obtained permission to leave the Jesuit order to join the congregation as Brother Andrew.

During the simple ceremony at the Shishu Bhavan in Calcutta, Mother Teresa gave Brother Andrew a small crucifix to be worn over his heart. It remains to this day the only distinguishing mark of the brothers of the Missionaries of Charity. In fact, it was Brother Andrew himself, with the agreement of Mother Teresa, who made the decision that the brothers should wear no uniform but only the everyday dress of laymen – trousers and shirts, such as poor people throughout the world might wear – and a crucifix to show their commitment to Jesus Christ. Brother Andrew was later to become the Superior of the Missionaries of Charity brothers.

Though an efficient and holy priest, this young man took pride in being called simply Brother Andrew. It was he who revised and updated the constitution of the Missionaries of Charity brothers. In Article 2, the special aim of the brothers is set down as follows:

> Brothers have to live this life of love by dedicating oneself to the service of the poorest of the poor in the slums, on the streets and wherever they are found. Leprosy patients, destitute beggars, the abandoned, homeless boys, young men in the slums, the unemployed and those uprooted by war and disaster will always be the special object of the brothers' concern.

As Superior of the brothers, Brother Andrew guided them and elevated them in all respects, and it is thanks to him that several houses of the Missionaries of Charity brothers were founded in different parts of India and abroad. As he put it himself, 'truly extraordinary circumstances' provided him with a house in Mansatala Row, Kidderpur, Calcutta, which was to become their headquarters.

It was President Kennedy who bought a few acres of land in the slum area of Dum Dum, Calcutta, and donated it to Mother Teresa and her brothers and sisters. The brothers ran a house there, where they looked after several boys. While the disabled studied at home, others were sent to local schools. Apart from that, the brothers also provided care and shelter for several people who were sick, disabled or destitute. The poor inmates of Dum Dum often get very good food to eat, because after every Air India flight, the left-over food is collected and brought there. It is a great source of satisfaction to see food being used up rather than wasted, and if you have felt the pinch of hunger, you will understand. Mother Teresa would make the point that we have sufficient fields around us to sow the seeds of goodness. We need only a little more goodwill and love for our fellow beings. 'Is it not a big sin to waste food,' she would ask, 'when our own brothers remain hungry and starving, craving for a mouthful of it?' And she would pray:

Make us worthy, Lord, to serve our fellow men throughout the world who live and die in poverty and hunger. Give them through our hands this day their daily bread, and by our understanding love, give peace and joy. Amen.

In February 1973, Brother Andrew opened a house in South Vietnam, where many poor and abandoned victims of the Vietnam War were helped. In 1974, he established another house of Missionaries of Charity brothers in Phnom Penh, and later he started branches of the brothers in the midst of the immense misery of Cambodia, and also in Taiwan, Hong Kong, South Korea, Los Angeles and other places.

He always said, and Mother Teresa agreed with him:

Mother Teresa and myself are just ordinary people. We have defects and deformities. On certain matters we do disagree and quarrel too, but only for that particular moment. God has chosen us. He made us tools to assist the poorest of the poor. But God is the ultimate cause of all goodness and success. So, it is God whom we thank and praise. I must say that Mother Teresa gave me total freedom, even when she disagreed with me.

Today there are nearly 400 brothers in the Missionaries of Charity, both in India and abroad, and among them are five priests. Those who come to join the brotherhood are not usually sent to study for priesthood, but it is fortunate to have a priest in a group of brothers, particularly in a place where there is no parish church.

On Belilious Road in Calcutta there is a Missionaries of Charity institution named Nabo Jibon, which is run by brothers. Some are given part of their training there, under the supervision of Brother Henry. Apart from that, they give proper care, including food, shelter and medicines, to nearly 100 male patients, both young and old. Nearly 200 street boys, all below sixteen years of age, who roam about day and night in the railway station and the bus stand of Calcutta and who have nobody on earth to give them a bit of love and care, assemble at Nabo Jibon every Sunday from 6 o'clock in the morning after Mass. They are attracted by sweet music and are free to sing or dance and to enjoy themselves. As the boys arrive, the brothers give them a thorough bath, wash their clothes and clean and dress their wounds. Most have some sort of injury, as a result of fighting, pickpocketing, stealing and other misdemeanours they get involved in daily.

The brothers are assisted by co-workers and volunteers, including nurses from different countries, who arrive there on Sundays to attend these boys at Nabo Jibon. Nowhere else do the boys get such care, offered with genuine love, compassion and affection. So instead of using bad language and fighting as they are accustomed to do, they sing and dance and make themselves cheerful after their baths. By noon, everybody is ready to queue for lunch, and they get as much food as they want to eat. After they have eaten, the boys leave, but any who are sick may remain to get special attention from the brothers.

Nabo Jibon is an ever-living and thrilling example that teaches us there are hundreds of ways and means to assist the poor. If you look around with a generous heart, you will always find some new way to serve people who need your attention and help.

———

At all times make it your aim to do good to one another and to all people. Be joyful always, pray at all times, be thankful in all circumstances. This is what God wants from you in your life in union with Christ Jesus. (I Thessalonians 5:15–18)

– 15 –

In the House of New Life

Some who come to Nirmal Hriday get a special blessing from God: the flame of life is almost extinguished, but the wick remains alight. When this happens, the sisters see it as their task to keep those wicks properly tended, cleaning them and pouring in fresh oil and using every possible means to keep them burning.

In order to look after these recovered people properly, Mother Teresa needed a separate place of safety and security where they could continue to be treated and helped towards a new life. With this ambition in her heart, she knocked at several doors, but not a single one was opened to her, until at last, in April 1973, ICI opened its door wide to her. This international company donated its large laboratory at Thiljala Road and its compound of five acres. What a wonderful gift! What a wonderful sign of great love for the poor!

Mother Teresa named it Premdan, and she entrusted responsibility for it to a dutiful and well-qualified nurse,

Sister Barbara, who had worked along with Mother Teresa, serving countless patients. Soon some of the patients from Nirmal Hriday were moved to Premdan and, before long, all the rooms there were filled with destitute people, whose bodies and minds had been crushed by illness and poverty. Unwanted by anyone, the sisters accepted them all and Premdan was soon throbbing with new life. These people are given not only a place to sleep, food to eat, clothes to wear and medicines to cure their illnesses, but also pure love, for which they thirsted. Food and medicines reach them without fail if they are unable to move from their beds, and the others come out onto the long veranda and receive food from the sisters there. It is the sisters who cook the food, wash up and keep the place clean.

There is a special ward in Premdan for those who are mentally ill. Even though these patients are unfortunate not to have a balanced mind, they can understand and enjoy the nectar of pure love. They can understand, as any animal does, the language of love, even though the people who work there express it in different languages. Moreover, they can reciprocate with a sincere smile – a smile that fills the hearts of those who give and receive with peace.

Once a mentally sick person got out of her room at Premdan, shouted and began to create problems. The sisters were afraid that she might attack Mother Teresa, who was weaker than the patient, and so they got hold of her to prevent her doing any harm. However, Mother Teresa was not at all afraid of the woman. She approached her, looked into her eyes and expressed her love and compassion with a smile. She put her weak hands on the sick woman's strong shoulders and the woman calmed down, looked at Mother Teresa as meekly as a lamb, and smiled. As Mother Teresa often told people, 'Peace begins with a smile.'

At one time, plenty of tender coconuts were available on the streets of Calcutta. After drinking the sweet water, people threw away the husks, which piled up everywhere in the streets, a constant headache for the Calcutta Corporation, which could not remove them quickly enough. The sisters from Premdan collected the husks and the healthy patients made useful materials from the coconut fibre to sell. Thus, the rubbish that the Corporation wanted removed from the street brought money to the poor inhabitants of Premdan. How happy they were to earn some cash from their own efforts! The Corporation too smiled along with them.

Coconut husks are no longer available, and so the sisters now collect used paper from offices. Every week, they distribute six kilos of paper each to selected families, who use it to make paper covers, which they then sell. For many a poor family, this is a great relief, as it provides work, which brings in money for provisions. The sisters also pick out paper on which there is still one clean side, which they use to make copybooks for poor students.

On 6 August 1997, Mother Teresa visited Premdan for the

last time. In fact, Premdan was the only institution she visited just before her death. At that time, 370 men and women were there. They knew that she loved them very much, and they were grief stricken when they heard, shortly after her visit, about her departure from this world.

Mother Teresa only needed to utter the word 'go' and her sisters or brothers would travel to any place she asked. She was ever convinced that the Almighty God who feeds the birds of the sky looked after the Missionaries of Charity brothers and sisters as well. And so, in July 1975, seven sisters reached Rourkela, where there is a large steel plant. They had no place to sleep and nothing to eat, but their hearts were full of love and longing to serve the poor, whatever hardship that might bring, even starvation. They went into the slum areas and served and adored Jesus, whose presence they found in the poor there. The selfless service and love rendered by the sisters was noticed not only by the local people, but also by the people in the steel plant, who immediately began to help them, in the first instance by letting them use one of their bungalows to sleep in. The local hospital gave the sisters all the necessary medicines required to treat lepers and students of the local school donated part of their pocket money, as well as a share of their food.

For the first ten months, the sisters had to struggle hard, but then there arose a new Premdan in Rourkela to give consolation and comfort to the poorest of the poor. The steel plant authorities donated two acres of land between two hills, where today this Premdan stands. Orphans go there, and physically and mentally disabled people, pregnant women who are homeless, the dying destitute, and those who suffer from incurable diseases.

Just as the people of the steel plant were generous in a big way, Mother Teresa often experienced equal kindness from people who had much less to offer but gave what they could with love. Once, a poor man on a bus offered his seat to her and, ignoring her protest, bought a ticket for her. Then, he opened a knot he had made on one end of the dhoti he was wearing and took out his savings. It was just a 10 paise coin. He gave it to her as if it were treasure and said, 'Mother kindly accept this coin too, I can do only this much for you.' She gladly accepted it and thanked him for his generosity. His poor mind filled with happiness and contentment, the reflection of which Mother Teresa could see on his face, for he had offered for the poor whatever he had, just like the poor widow who dropped her two little copper coins in the temple treasury. Mother Teresa prayed to God to bless that poor man abundantly.

———

I assure you that anyone who gives you a drink of water because you belong to me will certainly receive his reward. (Mark 9:41)

If the Great Leaders Shower Mercy

Mother Teresa had many friends in high places, who, because of their position, were often able to help her work. Dr B. C. Roy was a great friend of hers and he assisted her many times in the initial stages of her work, not by giving her money, but by showing her where she could get help, and he was the first political leader to publicize her work. On his eightieth birthday, when the Chief Minister was still in power, a reporter asked him what he thought about most of the time, and he replied, 'When I climbed the steps of this office today, my first thought was about Mother Teresa who has dedicated her entire life for the service of the poor and the destitute.' Next day, all the newspapers published his comment prominently on their front pages and many people were subsequently motivated to give help to their impoverished fellow beings.

Dr Roy asked Mother Teresa to take charge of four state-run homes for vagrants in Calcutta, but she refused because she could not spare the sisters. Even though she was friendly with the Chief Minister, she would not take on the big tasks he asked her to undertake, preferring to do her own work.

On another occasion, a reporter asked Mr Jyothi Basu, another Chief Minister of West Bengal, why he, as a Communist leader and an atheist, was so close to the well-known Catholic, Mother Teresa. He answered, 'There is a common factor that unites both of us: Mother Teresa and I love the poor.' Mother Teresa considered this to be true, because she received his whole-hearted support for many of her activities in Calcutta, without which it would not have been possible to treat so many lepers and to help so many poor and afflicted people there. She thought of Jyothi Basu as a true friend to whom she owed a great deal. During 1979, the International Year of the Child, the sisters organized a festival for 12,000 children at a stadium in Calcutta, to which an uninvited but very welcome guest arrived – Jyothi Basu. He would meet Mother Teresa any time, anywhere, and he gave orders that if ever she rang, she should be put straight through to him. Even at the busiest times, he would rush to visit her if he heard she was ill, and in 1983, when she was admitted to the Salvator Mundi Hospital in Rome after a heart attack, he sent a telegram to console her.

When Mother Teresa visited the local jail and met some female prisoners, she could not control her tears because they were living in such pitiable conditions. She spoke to Jyothi Basu, asking that the prisoners should be treated humanely, requesting lavatory facilities, food, clothing, medicines and so on, for some of them were actually going mad, so dreadful were the conditions. Mr Basu tried to wash his hands of this situation, as Pontius Pilate had done, saying, 'Mother, it is true that I am the Chief Minister of West Bengal, but I cannot do all that you do.'

She replied, 'Are they not our own sisters? Allow me to look after them. Grant me some land to rehabilitate them; can't you do that?'

She made her request with tears in her eyes and he was persuaded to grant her some land for this project. She could not rehabilitate the whole population of the prison, but she was able to take in more than 100 female prisoners who had become mentally or physically ill. The spacious building she acquired for this purpose was located at 24 Phargana, where the women were treated humanely under the care and protection of the Missionaries of Charity sisters.

Some of the prisoners wanted to visit their homes, and Mother Teresa obtained the necessary permission for them to do so from Mr Basu, but they all returned to the house within a month, as they were not accepted at home. Their relatives did not want a prostitute or a murderer or a criminal staying with them. On the contrary, they wanted to keep such people at a distance. However, Mother Teresa found that these ex-prisoners did not re-offend. Like the prodigal son, every one of them would return to the house, where they would get clean clothes, proper food, shelter and care. 'They are more hungry than ever for love,' Mother Teresa would explain, 'and we are ever ready to give it, and that is why they return to us without fail. *Thank God.*'

In 1960, Mother Teresa obtained permission to establish branches of her congregation outside Calcutta. The first house they had beyond the city was in Ranchi and later they established houses in Delhi, Jhansi and Agra. Prime Minister Pandit Nehru inaugurated their institution in Delhi, even though he was ill at the time. His love for the sisters was so great that he got up from his sickbed to join them at their function. When Mother Teresa tried to tell him about all their activities, he said, 'Mother, you need not tell me anything about your activities. I know them quite well; that is why I have come here today.' India had never honoured anyone born in a foreign country with Padmashree (one of India's top civilian honours), but Nehru recommended to the Indian President that Mother Teresa should be honoured in this way, an honour which she accepted in 1962 in the name of the poor people of India.

Establishing branches of her congregation in different parts of India helped Mother Teresa greatly in her work. Not only did the new branches flourish, but they also yielded plenty of good fruit, giving food, shelter and care to hundreds of sick, abandoned and unwanted poor. By 1981, they had institutions in sixty-eight centres.

Mrs Indira Gandhi was also a great friend of Mother Teresa's. Thanks to her magnanimity, the poor inmates of some of the Missionaries of Charity institutions used to get special food every now and then, for it was her standing instruction to send them whatever food was left over after every banquet held at Delhi. Mrs Gandhi also organized free passes for the railway and Indian Airlines. Mother Teresa was also much in debt to Mrs Gandhi for the favours she received from the government of India regarding customs and visas. And it was Mrs Gandhi, as Chancellor of Viswa Bharathi University, who offered her the Desikothama award. Mother Teresa had her doubts about the propriety of a university giving awards to a simple nun like herself, who lived and worked for the poor of India, but she accepted, in the name of the Lord Jesus. Also, she found that accepting such awards gave her a chance to talk about Jesus to some of the elite and the intelligentsia who would not hear about Him otherwise.

A certain Hindu association in Delhi arranged a reception for her at Red Fort, the historic Indian palace, after she received the Nobel prize in 1979. She had to attend, because the Prime Minister, cabinet ministers and other important dignitaries and government officers were at the function. Some of them remarked that she was the first Indian citizen after Pandit Nehru and Indira Gandhi to get an official reception at Red Fort. Mother Teresa was uncomfortable with this, as she felt that she had done nothing praiseworthy.

But since she had to speak a few words, she told them the following true story:

> One day when the sun was about to set, somebody rang my doorbell. I went and opened the door and I saw my Jesus in the shape of a poor leper. He was shivering with cold as he had nothing to cover his body and his stomach was empty. Immediately I arranged to give him some food and a blanket.
>
> However, that poor leper said with all his sincerity:
>
> > Mother, I have not come here today to get anything for myself. I heard the people say that you had received some big prize from somewhere. So, I too decided this morning that I would offer you as a present the entire alms I get today. I begged today from morning till this time and whatever I have got is in this alms plate. Mother, kindly accept it as my humble present.
>
> He extended his alms plate towards me as if he was offering all that he possessed. I accepted it, expressing my heartfelt gratitude. I counted the coins in the plate. It was altogether seventy-five paise. Even today you can see that seventy-five paise on my table. It reminds me how magnanimous human beings are!

Mr Rajiv Gandhi was also kind and helpful to Mother Teresa

when he was Prime Minister. A film director, a Mr Lapierre, wanted to make a film entitled *In the Name of God's Poor* in India, but he did not get the permission of the government to do so. However, Mother Teresa wrote on his behalf to Rajiv Gandhi, and he was kind enough to grant permission to Mr Lapierre on receiving her letter.

On 8 September 1989, Mother Teresa was admitted to the Woodlands nursing home in Calcutta following a heart attack and, shortly afterwards, she received a letter of consolation from Mr Gandhi. Moreover, he found time to visit her before she left the hospital. She never forgot this kindness, and she also remembered with gratitude how his wife, Mrs Sonia Gandhi, took the trouble to help the sisters by sending vegetables to the Shishu Bhavan at Delhi from time to time.

The terrible drought that affected Ethiopia in 1981 and the pitiable circumstances of the poor in that place troubled Mother Teresa's mind greatly. Some of the sisters rushed to Ethiopia with medicines, food and clothing, but their efforts only amounted to a teaspoonful of sugar in a big kettle of tea. The sisters returned to Calcutta and fasted for a day, praying to Almighty God to show them some way of helping the victims adequately. That night, in the midst of prayer, the name of Ronald Reagan, the President of America, came into Mother Teresa's mind, so she wrote him a letter. He contacted her by telephone as soon as he received it, and she explained to him the miserable situation of Ethiopia and requested him to extend a helping hand. He promised immediately to send urgent relief on behalf of the American people, as well as on his own behalf. He not only kept that promise within hours, but he also took the necessary steps to co-ordinate the entire relief work there.

On 28 October 1971, the sisters opened their first American institution in New York. Between 1976 and 1995 they established thirty-eight centres, including a novitiate, in different parts of the United States. Thus they were able to serve, love and care for many destitutes, including those who were suffering from AIDS. Hungry and thirsty, more for a little love than anything else, AIDS victims suffer even more hatred, abhorrence and isolation than lepers, but Mother Teresa would say that we are to remember that they too are the children of God. They too deserve our fraternal love and care and they too deserve to live like human beings, in peace and happiness. She would also say that we are not judges and it is not up to us to judge others. It is not difficult to find fault with others, but our mission is to assist them as far as we can, and our duty is to transform their last days of pain and agony into moments of acceptance, consolation, peace and joy.

In June 1985, Mother Teresa had the privilege of meeting AIDS patients at the George Washington University Hospital. Thanks to the help of Dr Richard Di Gioia, she was able to study the suffering of several of these patients. She could see that many AIDS victims were isolated and she wanted to help them. All that was required was a place to house them.

On 25 December 1985, the sisters opened a hospice for people afflicted with AIDS in Manhattan, the very heart of New York. Mother Teresa called it the Gift of Love and on the wall of that building hangs a poster where you can read the words she wrote at the age of seventy as her humble answers to the question, What is life?

Life is an opportunity, avail of it
Life is a beauty, admire it
Life is bliss, taste it
Life is a dream, realize it
Life is a challenge, meet it
Life is a duty, complete it
Life is a game, play it
Life is costly, care for it
Life is wealth, keep it
Life is love, enjoy it
Life is a mystery, know it
Life is a promise, fulfil it
Life is sorrow, overcome it
Life is a song, sing it
Life is a struggle, accept it
Life is a tragedy, embrace it
Life is an adventure, dare it
Life is life, save it

Life is luck, make it
Life is too precious, do not destroy it.

The Manhattan hospice was similar to the Nirmal Hriday in Calcutta, where patients received the love the sisters had to offer. A patient once said to Mother Teresa:

Mother, I had been living for the last twenty-five years without knowing God and without any sort of self-control. At last I reached this hospital and I found a new and true friend in you. From that day there was a total change in me. There was a change in my attitude towards my suffering.

I am suffering from severe headache, yet I bear it with joy and happiness, comparing it to the pain our Jesus suffered when the crown of sharp thorns was pressed deep into His head.

Similarly, I compare my intolerable backache to the pain Our Lord suffered when He was scourged; and the scorching pain of my hands and feet to that of Jesus when the nails pierced His hands and feet. When I suffer for Jesus and with Jesus, offering it in reparation for my sins, as you asked me to do, my pain becomes gain.

I have only one ambition: Mother, you must take me to your house. I want to die when you are near me.

Mother Teresa managed to obtain permission from the authorities and she took him to her chapel, where he had a sweet and uninterrupted conversation with Jesus, present in the sacrament. After three days he died in peace, a beautiful death.

To allow three young victims of AIDS in Sing Sing prison a similar peaceful and happy death, Mother Teresa pleaded with Mario Cuomo, Governor of New York, for their release. He kindly granted her request and within twenty-four hours the patients were moved to the Manhattan hospice.

On 13 June 1986, Mother Teresa met President Reagan at the White House. This meeting paved the way to the opening of another Gift of Love, in Washington, DC. She said to the President, 'I will do the praying and you will have to do all the rest.' Both he and the Most Reverend James Hickey, Archbishop of Washington, helped generously, and the Missionaries of Charity sisters were provided with twelve acres of land and the necessary buildings to accommodate and care for AIDS victims – men, women and children. 'We provided them with a loving home,' Mother Teresa said, 'where they could get the care, compassion, peace and joy they deserve, as the children of God, though they were suffering not only from AIDS, but also other terminal illnesses.'

By the grace of God, similar Gifts of Love sprang up in San Francisco in June 1988 and in Denver, Colorado, in 1989. Mother Teresa always remembered with gratitude how both President George Bush, Senior, and President Bill Clinton gave the sisters a helping hand and full co-operation in accomplishing this mission.

In the winter of 1970, Mother Teresa had been thinking of establishing a branch of her Missionaries of Charity congregation in England and, in no time, she and her sisters found what they were searching for – the poorest of the poor, exactly as in India. The people were in deep poverty and had no place of shelter, even to spend the cold nights. Some were trying to sleep in makeshift cardboard beds. Mother Teresa wanted to save them all, and to this end she later requested the assistance of Margaret Thatcher, the Prime Minister of the United Kingdom.

Mother Teresa was extremely shocked at what she saw in England. There were thousands who were about to drown in the pool of spiritual poverty. Hundreds were living a lonely life, having no one to look after them, and there were many who were spending the last days of their life in lonely, dark rooms as no one wanted them. Though she and her sisters had nothing, they told these poor people that they wanted and loved them.

One day the sisters came to the home of a woman who was living alone. A putrid smell emanated from the house as they rapped the door, but the woman refused to open it. Remembering the words of Our Lord, 'Knock and it shall be opened to you', the sisters persisted. Eventually, one of them was allowed in and found that the toilet the woman was using had been blocked and unusable days ago. As there was no one to help her, the other two rooms were also filled with faeces and urine. The sisters consoled her, went back outside and managed to find a shovel and a few bags. The sisters filled the bags with faeces and disposed of them. Then they washed and cleaned the rooms and the furniture, and within hours, the house was fit for a human being to live in.

The woman, who had remained silent, looked at the sisters with deep surprise and doubt and then she uttered solemnly, 'Do you still love me?'

'Of course we do,' said a sister with a broad smile, 'more than we did before.' Immediately God's love glowed and lit up her face with a sweet smile.

When Mother Teresa was in England, a humble idea sprouted up in her mind – it would be good to start up a novitiate house here. But where and how? After a long search, she found a suitable property, but the minimum price the owner was demanding was £9,000. How could she afford such a big amount? Without thinking about the pros and cons, Mother Teresa told the surprised owner that she could offer £6,000. She had a firm belief that if that place was suitable for the sisters, then Our Holy Mother would intervene, so she took a couple of medals of Our Lady from her bag and deposited them there.

A few days passed, and within that space of time, the owner of the house changed his mind. If he sold it to the sisters, he reasoned, although the price offered was ridiculously low, his house would be filled with the love of God! This thought gave him the sort of relief and consolation that money could not buy, and so he informed Mother Teresa that he was willing to sell at the silly price she had offered him.

But then the real problem emerged: where was the £6,000 to come from? Mother Teresa couldn't bring it from India, and how could she collect that much money in England? She prayed again to Our Holy Mother, and, as she prompted her, Mother Teresa travelled around England for a few days. She told everyone she met that she wished to start a novitiate house in England and that she needed some financial help. When the tour was over, Mother Teresa counted the money that had fallen into the cotton bag she carried: £5,995 pounds! And so she understood what God wanted her to do.

This was not an isolated incident. Many a sister has experienced several times that God does intervene with His wonderful providence in the affairs of the poor.

——

Look at the birds: they do not plant seeds, gather a harvest and put it in barns; yet your Father in heaven takes care of them!. (Matthew 6:26)

– 17 –

Trial by Ordeal

In 1970, God tested Mother Teresa in a way that not many others have experienced. She did not know that it was a serious test meant to measure her love for the poor. It all began with an unexpected letter from her sister, Aga, who wrote to her from Tirana:

The health of our beloved mother is deteriorating day by day. Similar is the condition of my health too. There is only one last desire left for our mother now. She wants to see her loving children, Agnes and Lazar, before she breathes her last.

Mother Teresa tried her level best to fulfil the last desire of her beloved mother, whom she had not seen for forty-two years, since she had bade her farewell from the train at Zagreb in 1928. The Lord Jesus was always with Mother

Teresa and He used to help her, even working miracles at times but, in this case, He left her on her own.

Accepting gladly the invitation of the Red Cross of Yugoslavia, she landed at Belgrade Airport on Wednesday, 8 June 1970. She was on her way to Jordan, to open a rehabilitation centre at Amman for Palestinian refugees. She travelled from Belgrade to Prizren, her ancestral home, and then to Skopje, just a few miles from Tirana. Skopje had been devastated by an earthquake in 1963, which had brought great suffering to many people. She visited the local bishop there, and afterwards she knelt before the statue of Our Lady at Letnice and prayed as she used to do when she was a little girl. She told Our Lady of her great desire to open a house of Missionaries of Charity sisters at Skopje.

Her plan was to go to Tirana to see her mother on her deathbed, in fulfilment of her last wish, but the Communist government would not give Mother Teresa permission to travel to Tirana. Utterly disappointed, she wept and offered her humble tears to God to accomplish His sweet will.

After the Second World War, her brother, Lazar, had taken refuge in Italy, escaping from the Communist government. Her mother and Aga longed to live with him and tried several times to get to Italy, but always in vain. The Communist government was stern and would not give them visas to leave Albania. This same government had closed down over 2,000 places of worship and misused more than 300 for other purposes. Priests were severely punished if they performed or even attended any religious function and more than 100 priests lost their lives due to persecution and torture, either in prison or in labour camps.

Mother Teresa wrote several times to the government of Albania, seeking permission to visit her native land, so that she might be able to accomplish the last desire of her mother. In reply to her repeated request, the Communist government eventually wrote: 'You will be permitted to go and see your mother. However, you shall not thereafter get an exit visa to leave Albania.' And so, for the sake of the poor all over the world, Mother Teresa abandoned her great desire to see her dying mother, her beloved Nonalok. She returned to Calcutta, where she heard by telegram that her mother had died on 12 July 1972 in Arans, Albania. Aga died a year later, in Tirana, on 25 August 1973.

In 1990 there was a change in attitude in the Communist government in Albania. The policy of persecution came to an end, and the wind began to favour those who believed in God and practised a religion. As an immediate effect, the government listened to Mother Teresa's humble request and allowed the Sacred Heart Church, which they had misused as a cinema, to be converted again to a place of worship. In 1991, two institutions of sisters were established at Tirana, one for the sick and destitute, the other for mentally and physically disabled children. The President of Albania himself gave permission, on 2 March 1991, for the opening of the Missionaries of Charity house there. People used to assemble in front of that first convent at Tirana, and Mother Teresa would tell them, 'We have come here to serve Our Lord and you. Yet, we require a little time for everything. Let us come to know first of all what you need urgently and then we shall act accordingly.'

The government had handed over two buildings to the sisters, one of which belonged to the Franciscan congregation. Mother Teresa repeatedly requested the government to return the building to that order and, as a result, the congregation had to be satisfied with another, smaller building. Nevertheless, they found there a great number of people who were really hungry for God. The government eventually allowed Mother Teresa to reopen six more churches. Meanwhile, she managed to get permission to reopen a former mosque, which the sisters got access to and cleaned thoroughly before handing it over to their Muslim brothers, who, ever since, have worked hand-in-hand with the sisters.

Something that had seemed impossible was now happening in the Communist country of Albania. Without explicit permission from the government, no one had been able to travel from place to place, or attend a family wedding, or meet any priest who had survived torture and persecution. Now all that had changed. 'Nothing is impossible for God!' was Mother Teresa's comment. In September 1991, Albania established relations with the Vatican, relations that had been cut off in 1945, and Archbishop Ivan Dias of Bombay took charge as the new nuncio to Tirana.

It gave Mother Teresa great happiness when the branches of her Missionaries of Charity congregation grew and spread out and began to yield plenty of good fruit at Tirana, Skhodra, Durres, Korce and Puke. Our Lord showed her another sign of His mercy, for she discovered that an anonymous person had been looking after the tombs of her beloved mother and her dear sister Aga in Tirana.

On 8 April 1976, the sisters established a branch near Colonia Santa Fe in Mexico, at the request of the President of Mexico himself. This was in a remote place, quite far from the city, where poverty, starvation and illnesses of various kinds had so conquered the poor that they hardly had any life in them. The sisters arrived, bringing what help they could, but they were extremely surprised to discover what the people really wanted. They did not ask for food, medicines and clothing, but they were hungry for God's love. They said, 'Sister, please talk to us about the love of God, for it is the love of God that brought you here.' What they said was quite true, as charity does not exist unless the love of God also exists. In fact, Mother Teresa would say, it is the love of God that takes the sisters to all sorts of places. If a calamity such as earthquake, drought, famine, flood, or flow of refugees occurs anywhere, the sisters come to know of it very soon, and they rush immediately to that place. They find out what the people need urgently, and they supply them with food, medicines and clothing. Members of other societies or associations involved in social or welfare work extend their helping hands to the sisters, and sometimes governments arrange helicopters to speed up the relief work. They all do what they can, so that the afflicted have their needs fulfilled.

The terrible typhoon and flood that occurred in Bangladesh in May 1991, for example, brought about tremendous destruction. Nearly 300,000 people perished. At that time, Mother Teresa was recovering from a heart attack, but she ignored the advice of her doctor and rushed to Bangladesh, collecting some of the medicines that were badly needed. The Prime Minister of Bangladesh, Begum Khalida, came to help her. The media gave good coverage to it, and all sorts of help flowed to the place of calamity from all corners of the world.

Mother Teresa wrote several letters to Mikhail Gorbachov, but she did not receive permission to go to the Communist USSR until there was a devastating earthquake, on 7 December 1988, in Armenia, resulting in terrible destruction and misery. Mother Teresa hurried to that place then, to undertake urgent relief work, collecting whatever she could in the way of medicines, clothes and equipment. After that, everything became much easier, and now the Missionaries of Charity sisters have fifteen centres in the former Soviet Union.

Even when it was almost impossible for a Christian congregation to get into northern Ethiopia, and at a time when hundreds of poor people were dying every day of dreadful drought and famine, Mother Teresa managed to arrange a meeting with the daughter of the Emperor Haile Selassie. She asked the princess, 'Are you not going to celebrate this week the forty-third anniversary of the coronation of the Emperor? Would you please inform your father that my sisters and I are ready to help his suffering subjects of Ethiopia as part of the celebration?'

The princess told her father what Mother Teresa had said, and he, in turn, sent his representative to her, who tried to silence her with questions, but he did not succeed.

She told him what he should say to the Emperor: 'We do not expect anything from the government. We give whole-hearted free service to the poorest of the poor and, working among the poor suffering people, we render compassion and tender love to the unwanted and the unloved.'

He asked, 'Do you preach to the people with the intention to convert them?'

She replied, 'That is not our intention, but our works of love reveal the love God has for them to the suffering poor.'

The next day the eighty-year-old Emperor granted Mother Teresa an audience and said to her, 'You are doing good works. I too have heard about them. Therefore I am very happy you have come. Yes, let your sisters come to Ethiopia.'

And so the Missionaries of Charity began their humble work at Addis Ababa, and later branches were established at Alamanta, Mek'ele and Gambella. Missionaries of Charity brothers also began work at Addis Ababa in 1986, and later a house was established at Gondar.

Three centres have been set up in Rome; the first started functioning at Via Casilina in 1980, another began that same year at Primavalle, and, in 1990, at Torree Bella Monacca. Mother Teresa was convinced that there were several of the poorest people even in the shade of St Peter's Basilica and that there was a necessity to set up a house in the Vatican, and she told His Holiness Pope John Paul II as much. The next time she visited the Vatican, she reminded His Holiness about this, and he, in turn, discussed the matter with others concerned and issued the order to find a suitable place, because, as His Holiness said himself, 'Mother Teresa will come here again and she will not forget to remind me about this matter.' And so, before her fourth visit to the Vatican, His Holiness had taken the decision to give her a beautiful house that had been built close to the hall that was used to welcome his guests. When she knelt down before him to receive his blessing, he presented her with the key of the new home of the congregation in the Vatican. This is how Mother Teresa described this occasion to her friends: 'Our poor people obtained some place even in the Vatican. From now on, the poor alone will be allowed to enter the Vatican, without taking an entrance ticket.'

Cassadona Di Maria is the name of the new building and here old women are given facilities to sleep at night. At 6 o'clock each evening, the door is opened. Those who are queuing outside are let in one after the other and are given their supper. This is what Sister Dorothy, who is in charge of Cassadona Di Maria, has to say:

We had to purchase almost nothing with money. In the beginning we used to go to the market and beg some vegetables, fish or meat. The people came to know what we were doing with them. Thereafter they started sending us whatever we needed.

Moreover, there are enough co-workers or volunteers who come to help us. Recordo is among them. He is a flight attendant at Alitta. He gets leave for two or three days after every flight. Yet, he spends the lion's share of that time of rest helping us at Cassadona Di Maria.

'A great miracle that is not at all a miracle!' was Mother Teresa's comment.

One evening, during a cold, wet spell of weather, somebody pressed the doorbell of Cassadona Di Maria. Sister Dorothy opened the door and saw a young man of sixteen or seventeen. He was wet and shivering and he asked, 'Sister, I am from Mauritius. Would you please give me a coat or jacket, so that I may escape from the severe cold?'

Before she could answer, she saw a big bag full of clothes nearby. There was a white jacket just on top of it. Pointing out that jacket, Sister Dorothy told him, 'Please take it and see whether it fits or not.'

The young man put it on. It fitted perfectly, as if it had been made for him. He and the sister looked at each other and smiled with great satisfaction.

As a matter of fact, Sister Dorothy did not know who had

left those clothes for the poor. Another little miracle, but also an ordinary event, the sort of thing that can happen in any Missionaries of Charity institution at any time. Food, clothing, money – they appear from somewhere without the knowledge of anyone when the poor people are badly in need of them.

The sisters in Rome used to go in search of the abandoned destitute. When they found them, they would give them all possible assistance and service. One day, they found an old man who had been alone in a room for a long time. They gave him all possible help.

After a few days he said, 'Sisters, you have brought God along with you! Now I request you to bring me a priest.'

Seeing his condition, the sisters brought a priest to the old man immediately. He began to wash his soul with tears of repentance and then made a good confession, thinking that it might be his last. He had not confessed for sixty years.

The very next day, with great joy and satisfaction, he slipped down to a peaceful sleep from which he never awoke. With the timely help of a priest, he captured heaven as the good thief who hung on the Cross on the right side of Jesus had.

———

Brethren and help are against time of trouble: but alms shall deliver more than them both. (Ecclesiastes 40:24)

– 18 –

Mother Teresa's Last Years

Priests had begun to work alongside the Missionaries of Charity as early as 1979. Reverend Father Joseph Langford had written to Mother Teresa about the idea that these priests should take the four vows of the Missionaries of Charity brothers and sisters, but it was a year and a half before she was convinced that this was the will of the Omniscient God. She was in Haiti at the time, and afterwards she spent four days with Father Langford in a contemplative house in the Bronx, New York, writing the statutes for the priest co-workers to present to the Holy Father.

It was from the Bronx that she flew to Rome to address the 202 bishops assembled there for the 1980 Synod. She said:

I do not feel worthy to speak in the presence of the Holy Father and the bishops, but I have accepted the invitation to come here so as to bring the request of all those who are rejected by society: the lepers, the poor, the dying, the sick, the forgotten and the abandoned. They have asked me to tell you that they need holy priests.

On 26 June 1981, His Eminence Cardinal Silvio Oddi and Archbishop Maximino Romero, the prefect and secretary of the Sacred Dicastery, Rome, wrote to her:

We wish to encourage wholeheartedly the movement 'Priest co-workers of Mother Teresa' . . . It is to be praised that the purpose of the movement, namely to live the Gospel more fully and faithfully, in greater simplicity and poverty of spirit, within the context of their own ministry and priestly vocation, by sharing spiritually in the charisma and spirit given by God to the universal church through Mother Teresa.

Father Langford had written about how the priest co-workers were to live together, how they should serve Jesus, present in the poorest of the poor, and Mother Teresa now presented this paper to the Holy Father. Though it was not practice for the Pope to sign anything then and there, he willingly signed this paper, writing on it: 'With my blessing, John Paul II, 17 August 1983.' He not only approved the formation of the priest co-workers, but also asked if he might become the first member of this congregation.

On 1 October 1983, Father Langford, along with two others, formed the congregation and started working in a house in the South Bronx provided by Cardinal Cooke of New York. They began to lead a renewed life absorbed in deep prayer, simplicity and charity. Two days later, Mother Teresa announced officially, 'Now we have Missionaries of Charity fathers in New York. This is a special gift given to us by God.' By and by, the movement of the priest co-workers grew and spread to sixty countries, where the priests loved and nursed Jesus, present in the very poor.

But this all happened after another important event in Mother Teresa's life. On the night of 2 June 1983, while she was in the convent of San Gregorio in Rome, Mother Teresa collapsed, and soon she found herself in the Salvator Mundi Hospital. Dr Vincenzo Bilotti, the famous heart specialist, examined her and found that she was suffering from severe heart problems. She wished to return immediately to the convent, but this could not be allowed. In fact, His Holiness Pope John Paul II ordered her by telephone, 'The entire world needs you, so please take rest.' Mother Teresa obeyed him, stayed in hospital, and cancelled all her plans. The only thing she could do now was a little suffering for the Lord Jesus, so she insisted that she would not take any pain-relieving drugs. Meanwhile, thousands of people all over the world prayed for her recovery, for which Mother Teresa was very grateful.

As soon as the doctor allowed her visitors, the King and Queen of Belgium were kind enough to come and console her. The President of India and many other people sent her flowers and cards. On 10 June, seven beautiful roses, representing the seven new Missionaries of Charity institutions opened that day, were sent to her by President Reagan. All these manifestations of love and affection provided her with new life and extra energy, that she was unable to stay in bed. So she sat in front of the statue of Our Holy Mother, opened the Bible and read the holy words, 'Who do you say I am?' (Matthew 16:15), then she wrote four pages of points of meditation on this verse for the future use of the brothers and sisters. Later, she told her sisters, 'We should be ever ready to act according to the decision, whatever it might be, taken by the Omniscient God about each one of us.' The exhortation 'Continue to serve Jesus, present in every suffering poor person' seemed to her the decision of the Lord with regard to her poor self, and so, even though she had severe backache, she went ahead with her plan to visit Germany, Poland, Belgium and USA.

Before she left the hospital, the doctors had given her a routine to follow and they entrusted her to the care and responsibility of Sister Gertrude. Accordingly, she was prohibited even to carry a baby in her arms or on her shoulders. She was also not allowed to attend public functions or to do any hard work. Sister Gertrude had been used to obeying Mother Teresa, but now Mother Teresa had to obey Sister Gertrude and, obeying her, she cancelled her planned visit to the United Kingdom that month.

When she was bedridden in Rome, she wrote and sang a

song, but she tore it up and put it in the wastepaper basket. She was not to know that Sister Stella Manippadam would retrieve it and give it to the inquisitive author of this book:

Jesus you are my God
Jesus you are my spouse
Jesus my life, my love, my all in all
Jesus word to be spoken
Jesus truth to be told
Jesus love to be loved
Jesus light to be lit
Jesus joy to be shared
Jesus peace to be given
You are God, God from God
Begotten not made.

Around this time, though she was busy opening new houses and finding sisters to run them, what Mother Teresa was most troubled about was poverty in Communist countries, where the people were not only materially but also spiritually poor. Some had never heard that God was Our Father and that He loved all men on earth. 'Don't I have some obligation to show them a little light to save them from the darkness of such ignorance?' Mother Teresa reasoned. 'How long shall I sit idly on the pretext of my poor health? How can you sit in a chair when you are caught in a fire?' And so she went ahead and opened a new house at Karl-Marx-Stadt in East

Germany, in December 1983. Then, in response to the request of Cardinal Joseph Glemp, she visited Poland the following year, but she had to return to Salvator Mundi Hospital afterwards.

Mother Teresa would often count the blessings that God's mercy showered on the Missionaries of Charity brothers and sisters. It was by His grace that, in 1984, they were able to treat 4 million lepers through the mobile clinics; distribute rations to 106,271 people; serve cooked food to 51,580 people through relief centres; bring to Nirmal Hriday and tend 13,246 dying destitute; and save 8,627 people from imminent death. They were also able to look after over 6,000 babies in their 103 Shishu Bhavans. Mother Teresa was grateful, not only to God, but also to the hundreds of co-workers and volunteers who generously extended their helping hands to the brothers and sisters in doing all this work.

Also in 1984, she formed an association of doctors in Rome. Most humbly she told them:

Medicine is a gift and blessing given by God. Keeping that in mind, the patients are to be loved and respected before God and man. The sick and suffering people don't need pity, they need our love and compassion. Because the sick, the lonely and the disabled come to you with hope, they must be able to receive from you tender love and compassion.

By the grace of God, most of the doctors assembled there willingly came forward to be members of the medical co-workers of the Missionaries of Charity. Also in that year, Mother Teresa wrote a letter to all the co-workers over the world and in it she said:

I earnestly request you, all doctors in the various countries, with my folded hands, not to pursue purely the material goals, but to give some of your precious time for helping to improve the lot of the poor.

She entrusted Dr Francesco Di Raimondo, a senior physician of the Lazzaro Spallanzi Hospital in Rome, and his wife Gabriella, with the responsibility of being the international links for the medical co-workers, which they undertook in a most praiseworthy manner. Without any discrimination on grounds of caste, creed or colour, doctors, nurses, pharmacists and others, professionally committed to health care from different parts of the world, joyfully joined the group of medical co-workers and volunteered their valuable service free of charge to help the Missionaries of Charity. Within four years, this association spread worldwide and became a source of strength and protection for the diseased and discarded.

On 31 October 1984, Mother Teresa's dear friend, Prime Minister Indira Gandhi, was assassinated, and Mother Teresa returned to India to pray for her and to attend her cremation, and also to work among the Sikh refugees who needed help because of the violence that erupted after the assassination.

As Christmas 1984 approached, Mother Teresa came to hear of the terrible famine in Africa. She had a mild fever at the time but, in spite of this, she travelled there. The Missionaries of Charity had five houses in Africa and she co-ordinated the relief work with the help of the sisters there. In Addis Ababa, she met the rock singer Bob Geldof, who presented her with £6 million, which he had raised through rock music for the relief of famine in Ethiopia. Mother Teresa was deeply grateful to him.

On 20 January 1985, Mother Teresa first set foot in China. The sisters had houses in Macao, South Korea and Hong Kong, and Mother Teresa spent a few days in Macao and Korea before going to Hong Kong and then on to China. Another Nirmal Hriday was established in Hong Kong, in a building provided by the government.

The Chinese government was of the opinion that there were no poor people in China, but Mother Teresa visited a home for the aged in Beijing and also a factory for disabled workers, where she shared God's love, giving them comfort and consolation. Since there was no surviving convent in China, there was no convent for her to stay in overnight, which was what she usually did when she was travelling, and instead she had to be put up in a high-rise hotel. From there she prayed for all her Chinese brothers and sisters, and especially for the poor.

Mother Teresa had to cancel a visit to Japan in March 1987. She was not allowed to travel because of her heart problem and, in her message to the people there, she said that they should 'love one another as God loves each one'. When she was allowed to travel again, new houses were opened in Africa, Cuba and Russia.

From 1989, her health began to deteriorate considerably. She had to send representatives to the places she had promised to visit, but the moment she got permission to travel again, she flew, with five sisters, to Budapest on 18 June of that year, and eventually branches of the sisters came into existence in the Hungarian capital and in Erd. When she returned to Calcutta the following month, she discussed with her sisters how they could help the destitute poor of Peru, Switzerland and Albania and they made arrangements to open a Missionaries of Charity house in Albania, as soon as possible, and two houses were established in Tirana in 1991.

On 3 September 1989, Mother Teresa's health again deteriorated. High fever, nausea, chest pain and fatigue increased so much that, two days later, she asked for the last sacrament. She was moved to Woodlands nursing home in Calcutta, but on 8 September, her condition took a turn for the worse. The Holy Father, Pope John Paul II sent her a message:

Commending you to the intercession of our loving Mother Mary, help of the sick, I cordially impart my special Apostolic Blessings as a pledge of strength and comfort in Our Lord and Saviour, Jesus Christ.

Similar messages of sympathy, prayers and blessings reached her from the President of India, Mr Venkaitaraman, and Prime Minister Rajiv Gandhi. They all gave her consolation as well as encouragement.

Soon, Dr Vincenzo Bilotti, who had attended her in Rome, reached Calcutta. He fitted an external pacemaker and brought her irregular heartbeat under control. Her niece Aggi came to see her, and her close friend, Ann Blaikie, flew to Calcutta, embraced her with tears in her eyes and consoled her. Rajiv Gandhi also came, along with other important people. In short, Mother Teresa's suffering brought the entire world to prayer.

By the grace of God she was released from the hospital on 14 October, but was admitted again on 29 November. A more permanent pacemaker was fitted and she was discharged on 11 December, with a strict warning to reduce her workload.

President Yasser Arafat met her in Calcutta on 28 March and invited her to the Holy Land. He asked her to open 'Death with Dignity' homes, similar to Nirmal Hriday, in Jerusalem and Bethlehem, promising her $50,000. She did not know what to do, since she was so ill. She had written to the Holy Father:

Due to health reasons, herewith I am submitting my resignation as the Superior General of Missionaries of Charity. Kindly grant me the permission to choose my successor so that the work of the congregation may go on without interruption.

On 11 April 1990, His Holiness reluctantly accepted Mother Teresa's resignation and before the chapter of 1990 in which the election for her successor was to be held, she wrote a letter to all the members of the Missionaries of Charity – sisters, brothers, priests and co-workers.

This brings you my prayer and blessing for each one of you – my love and gratitude to each one of you, for all you have been and have done all these forty years to share the joy of loving each other and the poorest of the poor . . . We are nothing. God has shown His greatness by using nothingness and doing miracles . . . Let us accept whatever He gives and give whatever He takes with a big smile . . .

When the chapter was over, what she had written to the sisters came back to her like a boomerang, when they re-elected her. She was over eighty years old by then, but she reasoned that she had to take whatever He gives. The Holy Father and all the rest were very happy about it. Mother Teresa bowed to the will of the Lord Jesus and repeated what she had said to a US senator, 'God has not called me to be successful. He has called me to be faithful.'

——

And thy counsel who hath known, except thou give wisdom, and send thy Holy Spirit from above. (Wisdom of Solomon 9:17)

– 19 –

The Miracle that is the Missionaries of Charity

It was the Lord Jesus, Mother Teresa always maintained, who drew the picture of the Missionaries of Charity with the pencil that was Mother Teresa. In 1990, she looked at that picture and found it was miraculous indeed.

First she saw the miracle of the number of applicants to the Missionaries of Charity increasing each day. By 1990, she saw that 3,068 sisters had taken their final vows, and there were 454 novices and 140 new candidates, and novitiate houses not only in Calcutta, but also in Manila, Rome, Poland, San Francisco, Tabora and Tanzania. Moreover, a novitiate house had been established in New York especially for the contemplative branch of the order. Missionaries of Charity convents, numbering more than 400, had been opened in ninety countries. From February 1965, the congregation had been under the direct control of

His Holiness the Pope, which made recruitment and growth easy to achieve.

The Missionaries of Charity brothers also had novitiate houses in, amongst other places, Calcutta, Vijayawada, Manchester, Los Angeles, Seoul and Manila. Brother Andrew, who had been a lamp to the feet of the brothers, left the congregation in November 1987, went to his native Australia and became involved in other missionary activities. Brother Geoff was elected in his place as Superior General. There were, by this time, 380 professed brothers in eighty-two houses in twenty-six countries, doing similar work to that carried out by the sisters.

A new community of the Missionaries of Charity fathers, set up in 1983, was still quite small, but it had branched out in several countries. Under the special guidance of Father Joseph Langford, they were doing wonderful work at Tijuana in Mexico. As early as 1989, they had nine priests and thirty-three seminarians.

In 1990, Mother Teresa was extremely happy to note that there were more than 3 million co-workers all over the world doing small things with great love, just like the brothers and sisters. In 1981, Mother Teresa had founded the Youth Co-workers, and these young people had great manpower and ability 'to quench the infinite thirst of Jesus for love'. She was also happy to see that the Medical Co-workers, begun in 1984, had already spread to all five continents by 1990.

In 1989, another branch, the Lay Missionaries of Charity,

came into being. Here, lay people, married or unmarried, live in accordance with each one's own state of life, keeping vows of chastity (conjugal chastity in the case of married members), poverty and obedience, as well as wholehearted and free service to the poor. They take the Holy Family of Nazareth as their model of life. Their lives and work provide an edifying example and an incentive to the other co-workers of the locality in which they dwell.

Even in Communist countries, where the existence of God was for so long obstinately denied, the Missionaries of Charity have spread the love of God. Five convents began functioning in the Soviet Union during the summer of 1990: two each in Moscow and Armenia and one in Georgia. On 30 April 1990, the sisters opened a home in Bucharest for children suffering from AIDS and, on 13 May, two convents were established in Czechoslovakia. In His mercy, Mother Teresa was able to look after and tend the destitute after purchasing some land and starting a convent in Tirana. The people who believed in God thronged there to meet Mother Teresa, and she announced, to their joy and satisfaction, 'As we do all over the world, we have come here too, to give you tender love and care. We will begin slowly and find out what is your greatest need.' Before long, she brought a few more sisters from Rome to Albania and opened three houses there, one after the other. Ramis Alia, the President of Albania, was so satisfied with the humble service of the sisters that he granted Mother

Teresa citizenship of Albania in 1992, and permission to come and go whenever she pleased.

There are also four convents in Cuba, and indeed President Fidel Castro requested Mother Teresa to open three more. In the district of Josefstown, God Almighty enabled the sisters to give a meal a day to the elderly, the physically or mentally disabled, and the homeless. Mother Teresa would always plead with everyone she met to feed just one poor person daily. 'Don't forget,' she would say, 'that God will reward you a hundredfold if you give away something that God has given you freely.'

In 1992, a request came from Baghdad for help to alleviate the suffering of the poor, brought about by the terrible war in Iraq. The sisters went there immediately and helped the people who were faced with famine, drought, disease and all other maladies of war. By the grace of God, they found a suitable place in the heart of Baghdad itself. No sooner had they cleaned the place up than it was filled with malnourished and crippled children and dying destitute. Mother Teresa wrote on 23 June of that year: 'There is so much suffering everywhere! I never thought that our presence would give so much joy to thousands of people.' Because of war, there were many old and sick and those who were unable to walk. How could the sisters get the necessary help to them? This problem was solved when the Iraqi government gave them a vehicle, which they used as a mobile clinic and to bring food, water and medicines to the people.

Mother Teresa wrote to her brothers and sisters:

Give whatever God wants and accept whatever He gives
with a big smile. This is what I mean by total surrender to
God. Thus, let us make ourselves empty so that He might
fill us with Himself and His love. Then we will be free. I
ask you but one thing. Be a true Missionary of Charity
and so satiate the thirst of Jesus for love of souls by working at the salvation and sanctification of your community,
your family and the poor you serve.

Mother Teresa arrived in Washington, DC, in December
1991, and participated in a function in which twenty-seven
sisters made their final vows. She met President George Bush,
senior, and they discussed some of her future plans. She then
left for Tijuana, from where she paid a brief visit to Los
Angeles to open a new house. The sisters in Los Angeles
were suffering from flu, and Mother Teresa became infected
by the virus before she returned to Mexico. On 26
December, it was announced that she was suffering from
pneumonia. Although she wanted to be treated in the local
hospital in Tijuana, she was taken instead to the Scripps
Clinic in California, where angioplasty surgery was performed to clear her clogged arteries.

In February 1992, Mother Teresa went to Rome, where she
met for the last time her long-standing friend and co-worker
Ann Blaikie, who was also suffering from illness. During this

trip, Mother Teresa slipped and broke three ribs. Sister Gertrude, in whose absence this accident occurred, rushed to her side. Mother Teresa reproached her with a smile, saying, 'You see what happens to me when you leave?' The moment she made some recovery, her unbroken spirit urged her to go ahead with her plans.

On 31 May, she travelled to Dublin and, on 1 June, she spoke what was in her mind to those who assembled:

> Our Lady loves Ireland. So, let us make a strong resolution that in this beautiful country no child may be unwanted. Let us promise to Our Lady that we will never have a single abortion in this country and that there will be no divorce in this country . . .

Mother Teresa's humble efforts to provide a shelter for people sleeping on the streets in London succeeded on 7 June, when she opened a 35-room hostel for the homeless. She was very grateful to the managers of the *Daily Mirror* and the *Sunday Mirror* who had raised £300,000 by an appeal launched for this purpose.

She reached Delhi in August 1993 to receive an award from the Indian government for 'promoting peace and communal harmony'. But, as she was suffering from fever, vomiting, congestion of the lungs and breathlessness, she was taken immediately to the All-India Institute of Medical Science, where, once again, she had to undergo a heart operation, and once again thousands of people prayed for her day and night. Her heart problems recurred in mid-September. People began to pray for her again and Pope John Paul II sent her a message of goodwill. Father Celeste Van Exem, Mother Teresa's beloved spiritual adviser, wrote her what was to be his last letter on 16 September:

Dear Mother,

Tomorrow morning I shall say Holy Mass for the following intentions:

That you may have no operation.
That you may be in China by 7 October 1993.
That the Lord may take me and not you if that is His will. His will, not mine.

I am with you and the sisters, all of them. There is a Calvary for every Christian. For you the way to Calvary is long. But Mary has met you on the road. You did not go up the hill; this is for later.

I adore the Blessed Sacrament which, I am sure, you have in your room. Pray for me and all my companions, especially the Companions of Jesus with whom I am.

Yours sincerely in O.L.
C. Van Exem, SJ

Just four days after writing this letter, Father Van Exem

passed away. Mother Teresa was unable to attend his funeral, but she saw his body from the window of the convent where she stood with Sister Nirmala, as it was being carried to St John's cemetery from St Xavier's College. 'Let his soul rest in peace,' she prayed, and she said to Sister Nirmala, 'I am sure that he was very holy. He has gone straight to God.'

As Father Van Exem had wished, Mother Teresa was soon well enough to go to China. Her ambition was to open a house at Shanghai for disabled children, but she found that she needed more time to accomplish this, as well as ardent prayer. She attended final vows ceremonies on 8 and 9 December in Rome, and then she visited Poland before returning to India.

Accepting an invitation from President Clinton, she attended a meeting in Washington, DC, on 3 February 1994. The speech she delivered there against abortion went against the views held by most of the dignitaries present. Yet, by the grace of God, she was able to open a home for unwanted children in the city on 19 June 1995.

She had travelled again to China in March 1995 and met several people, but her desire to open a home for the destitute there was not fulfilled. She went to Vietnam, where she opened two more Missionaries of Charity houses.

Mother Teresa very much wanted to attend ceremonies held in different parts of the world where fifty-two of her sisters were taking their first vows and seventy-six their final vows, but she was curtailed by poor health, so she wrote to them instead:

We have already spread to different countries now and I wish to be present at the blessings of these new taber-nacles. Yet, it is physically impossible for me to do so. Hope you will kindly excuse me.

On 1 April 1996, she was again admitted to the nursing home. Her collar bone had broken the previous night when she had fallen from her cot. She joked with some of the sisters who attended her, 'My guardian angel pushes me down somewhere or other whenever he finds that I am running up and down without taking proper rest.' This incident led to the cancellation of all the programmes she had planned, but she was soon able to go to America, Rome and Ireland, as the need to do so motivated her. But she slipped again and fell down a staircase in Dublin, and found herself once more in a wheelchair. She managed, all the same, to go to Armagh in Northern Ireland in June 1996 to inaugurate a new house there, and then, before returning to Rome, she stopped first in London, by which time she was able to abandon her wheelchair and walk again, and then in Swansea she opened the 565th Missionaries of Charity house on 18 June, thanks to Sister Nirmala, who was her right-hand woman during this whole trip.

Mother Teresa was re-admitted to Woodlands, and by the

end of August, she was unable to breathe without the help of a respirator. On hearing this news, Sister Nirmala flew from New York, and the entire world began to pray for her. Yet again, Mother Teresa regained consciousness and her temperature came down. When her eighty-sixth birthday arrived, the sisters assembled in the hospital to celebrate it, and they witnessed a miracle: Mother Teresa was breathing properly without the assistance of the respirator. It was also a matter of wonder even for those who had been treating her. She told the doctors, 'My health and my life are in the holy hands of the Almighty.' They listened to her request and discharged her from the hospital on 6 September.

Tuesday, 10 September 1996 was the Golden Jubilee day of her second vocation, the day she called her Inspiration Day. Sister Agnes, Sister Gertrude and many other sisters surrounded her but, to their disappointment, Mother Teresa declared, 'Let us have no celebration today. Instead, let us spend the day in deep meditation followed by thanksgiving to Our Lord Jesus.' On 16 September, she was overcome by dizziness and collapsed, and once more she was hospitalized. But by the 25th, she appeared to be happy and quite energetic, so she was discharged from hospital.

On 22 November, Mother Teresa again experienced sudden and severe chest pains, which lasted throughout Saturday and Sunday. The heart specialists began treatment and, within a week, they had operated on her heart and again cleared her arteries. People all over the world of different castes and creeds – Hindus, Muslims, Christians and Buddhists – prayed to God for her recovery. She wanted to return to her convent on 4 December but she was not allowed to leave the hospital until Thursday 19 December. On that day she walked, without help, to the car and was taken to the convent. She suffered unbearable back pain, but she did not disclose it to anybody, and instead offered it up to the Lord Jesus. Even so, she had to take bed rest.

It was now time to elect a new Superior General of the congregation. In preparation for this, the sisters went on a retreat. His Grace Dr Henry D'Souza, Archbishop of Calcutta, informed the sisters before they began the chapter of Mother Teresa's desires and intentions: she wished 'to resign as the Superior General of our congregation of Missionaries of Charity. On no account shall I allow a repeat of what happened in 1990. Hence you have to elect certainly my successor in the ensuing chapter.' By letter, the Holy Father exhorted the 123 delegates who had assembled in Calcutta to 'pray in a special manner to elect a successor to Mother Teresa in the next chapter, in accordance with the sweet will of the Omniscient God'.

The election result was finally announced on Thursday 13 March 1997, and it was Sister Nirmala, the former head of the contemplative sisters, who was elected Superior General. Sisters Frederick, Priscilla, Lysa and Martin De Porres were elected councillors.

Nirmala Joshi was a member of a middle-class Hindu

Brahmin family who had settled at Doranda near Ranchi in Bihar. When she was studying in the Women's College at Patna, she used to watch one of her friends kneeling down and praying in front of the crucifix. Slowly she was attracted towards Jesus and she could get all her doubts cleared through that good friend; and that is how she found Jesus and Jesus found a place in her heart. She joined the Missionaries of Charity in 1958 and became a sister in 1961. From 1979, Sister Nirmala was in charge of the contemplative wing and led the sisters in a most praiseworthy manner. It was Sister Nirmala who took the lion's share in establishing one of the houses in Venezuela. Mother Teresa maintained that she was a great treasure God Almighty had made plans for earlier and kept for the congregation, though she was born and brought up in a Hindu family and became a Catholic only at the age of twenty-three, after completing her higher education. 'She is far better than me in humility, devotion to God, education, wisdom and in love of God and love of fellow beings,' Mother Teresa declared. 'I am extremely glad that God has chosen her as our Superior General.'

When reporters asked Sister Nirmala whether she considered herself to be the right person to assume the foundress's awesome mantle, she made a most befitting answer, 'The Lord will make me fit for the job, if you pray for me.'

Mother Teresa would often say that the secret of the success of the Missionaries of Charity brothers and sisters is the mentality of offering everything to the Lord Jesus, just as Sister Nirmala expressed in her answer.

As head of the contemplative sisters, Sister Nirmala loved and kept silence for a long time. These were Mother Teresa's words about silence:

> God is the friend of silence,
> If we really want to pray,
> We must first learn to listen, for
> In the silence of the heart God speaks.
> The fruit of the silence is prayer,
> The fruit of the prayer is faith,
> The fruit of faith is love and
> The fruit of love is silence.
> Let us use love and compassion to overcome the world.

And so the congregation's anxiety about finding a successor had come to an end, and Mother Teresa humbly requested everyone, inside and outside the congregation, to give Sister Nirmala the same support they had always given to her. They were now to give Sister Nirmala the same love, prayers, help and co-operation that they had showered upon her so lavishly.

By 2001, the congregation of the Missionaries of Charity was functioning in 123 countries, rendering selfless service to the poor and, in particular, to orphans, destitute, diseased, and mentally and physically disabled people, and the victims of AIDS and leprosy. They had more than 3,500 sisters, about 400 brothers, 2,000 mission workers, 169 educational institutions, 1,369 clinics and 755 convents, excluding the leprosy relief centres, Shishu Bhavans and so on, which are attached to them. Mother Teresa asked for prayers to the Lord Jesus to bless Sister Nirmala abundantly, to enable her to run everything in the best way possible and to bring them to the highest degree of growth, in respect of size, reach, spirituality and holiness.

The Lord Jesus always gave Mother Teresa crosses to bear throughout her life, as well as supporting her. One of these crosses was the cancer that inflicted unbearable pain on her beloved Sister Agnes, who had been her right hand from the very inception of the congregation. On 9 April 1997, while the sisters were offering a last Mass at Sister Agnes's bedside, she offered her sufferings to God and left for her heavenly home to prepare a room for Mother Teresa.

When Mother Teresa arrived in Rome on 16 May to officially introduce Sister Nirmala as the new Superior General to His Holiness, he was already aware of her ill health. However, she was well enough to discuss with the Holy Father the possibility of rehabilitating prostitutes in the run-down areas of Rome, and to participate in the ceremony of the profession of a number of new sisters.

All this time, she was carrying another cross, namely her difficulty in breathing, for which she had to take oxygen two or three times a day. Because of her delicate condition,

Mother Teresa was forced to cancel a visit to Poland, but she went ahead with her visit to the United States, where she attended the profession of some of the sisters, whom she congratulated. This, in turn, gave her some strength and, to the great astonishment of many, people saw her frail body walking in the Bronx, hand in hand with the energetic Princess Diana and smiling at everyone she met. Well, peace begins with a smile, as she used to say.

The sisters wanted Mother Teresa to celebrate her eighty-seventh birthday in the mother house in Calcutta, and so she returned to India to fulfil their wish. It was to be her last birthday celebration here on earth.

How wonderful are the things the Lord does! All who are delighted with them want to understand them.
(Psalm 111:2)

– 20 –

Mother Teresa's Last Day

On 5 September 1997, a First Friday, a day specially dedicated to the Sacred Heart of Jesus, Mother Teresa got up at her usual time, offered everything to the Sacred Heart, said her morning prayers in her room, and then went to the chapel for Mass. After Mass, some poor afflicted and abandoned people, the people Mother Teresa had spent her life caring for, were waiting outside to meet her. Among them were a father and mother weeping with unbearable sorrow, for they had lost their only daughter to suicide, and they did not understand why she had done it. Mother Teresa consoled them as best she could, staying some time with them, and then she went to breakfast and to open her post.

Later, she attended a council meeting of the sisters, but she was much agitated and wanted to finish the meeting quickly. At last she was able to return to her room, where she spent some time writing thank you messages. When she had finished a box of cards, she asked Sister Joyal for some more, but

Sister Nirmala told Mother Teresa that she was doing too much and she should rest. Mother Teresa did not want to rest. She wanted to get on with the work and, in the end, Sister Nirmala silently assented.

Mother Teresa went on writing cards until noon, when she had some lunch. Normally she would fast on a First Friday, but she was not allowed to do that today and so she obeyed doctor's orders. She joined in community prayer after lunch, and then she tried to take a rest, but her back ached and she could not sleep. The sisters knew she was not well and did not allow any visitors to disturb her, and so she was alone with her thoughts and her prayers, keeping her rosary always in her hand.

When it came time for the Way of the Cross, Mother Teresa left her room, met some people who were waiting to see her and gave them medals of Our Lady. She spoke to others on the phone, signed some letters, met some sisters, and even met the film star Sashikala, who had made a change in her way of life.

A great tiredness came over Mother Teresa and she lay down again. She felt that Jesus was asking something of her, and so she got up and stood, asking, 'What is it? What does Jesus want of me?' Her mind was in conversation with Jesus, but her body was racked with pain. Sister Nirmala came and helped her back to bed and later brought her tea and biscuits. She left Mother Teresa again for a while with her spiritual reading, while she spoke to some people who were waiting to meet her. When she came back, Mother Teresa reproached her gently, 'You have forgotten Mother today, haven't you?' Sister Nirmala smiled her sweet smile and said she had not forgotten her at all.

By now it was four o'clock, time to go to the chapel for adoration. Mother Teresa wished to join them, but when she tried, she found she could not, for the pain in her back was almost unbearable. She lay down again, and then someone told her that Brother Geoff, who was to fly that night to Singapore, wanted to see her. She put aside her pain, sat in her chair, and received him. He told Mother Teresa all his plans, and she asked him to convey her love to the brothers and sisters he would meet on his trip.

Then, keeping her hand on her chest and looking straight into his eyes, she declared, 'As you all know, I do not find any difference between our brothers and sisters. Never. The only difference is this: you stay there, in your building, and we stay here.' She looked across her desk to the picture of the Sacred Heart that hung over it, in a handsome frame. It was a picture she often looked at and kissed. It suddenly came to her that this would be a good gift to give to her beloved brothers, and so she took the picture down and offered it to Brother Geoff as a memento, as if she had no further need of it. It was a small gesture, but that last, loving gift to the brothers is held dear by them all over the world.

Brother Geoff said goodbye to her, and Mother Teresa

said, 'I will be with you in spirit always at any place wherever you go, assisting you with my prayers.'

After he left, she lay down again. The adoration was over in the chapel, and the sister in charge of the Holy Eucharist brought it to Mother Teresa in her room. She kissed her Lord Jesus, present in the sacrament, for the last time.

Mother Teresa had an appointment to meet officials of Indian Airlines, but she was unable to get up from her bed. Sister Nirmala went to them instead and conveyed Mother's love and best regards. Several people were waiting to meet her, but all she could do was wave at them from a distance. She was unable to go to the chapel for prayers, and could only join in from her room.

Sister Gertrude was with her now, and Mother Teresa joked with her, 'My right leg is extremely jealous of my left leg, for it is left out in the matter of getting some relief. Apply the medicines, kneading, massaging – the entire relief measures are given only to the left leg.'

Sister Gertrude laughed and started to attend also to Mother's right leg. Then Mother Teresa asked Sister Gertrude to go to the chapel on her behalf, since she could not go herself, and so Sister Gertrude obeyed, giving Mother Teresa her crucifix before she left.

Sister Nirmala came then to sit with her, and they said the Rosary together and also the other prayers they usually said on Fridays, as well as the prayer to the Sacred Heart in reparation for their sins. Then, without looking at the book,

Mother Teresa sang the hymn 'Sweet Lord Jesus'. By now the prayer was coming to an end in the chapel, and she could hear the sisters singing a hymn to Our Holy Mother. It was time to eat now, and she said the prayers before supper.

Sisters were rushing up and down, busy with various tasks, and for a while Mother Teresa was alone, speaking quietly to Jesus, not noticing the time passing. All of a sudden, she called out, 'Sisters, I cannot breathe!' The sisters came running to help, bringing oxygen and medicines, and someone called the parish priest and the doctor.

The agony of death was upon Mother Teresa. Her last action was to lift her hand and touch and kiss the crucifix, offering her sufferings along with those of Jesus, and all the while whispering, 'Jesus, I love you. Jesus, I offer myself to you. My God, I thank you, praise you and adore you. Jesus, I love you . . .'

By now there were several sisters around her, and Father Hansel, the parish priest of St Mary's, came to her and she received the Anointing of the Sick, which would cleanse her soul and make it fit to enter heaven. Meanwhile, Dr Woodland had also arrived, and he and Sister Gertrude were trying their best to steady Mother Teresa's heartbeat. Nobody was willing to admit that she was finally going.

Somebody cried out in anxiety, 'Mother is dying.'

Sister Joyal went to her side, and heard her whisper, 'Jesus, I love you. Thank God. Thank God.' The words she had so often repeated were on the tip of her tongue, but she was starting to lose the strength to say them. Sister Gertrude noticed this, and so she took up the words and spoke them into Mother Teresa's ear, so that she could repeat them in her mind.

Even though the people around her could see that she was sinking, they found it hard to believe that Mother Teresa was finally going to her Creator, for she had been talking, laughing, praying until eight o'clock that evening. They expected that, as had happened so often before, her heartbeat would return to normal and she would begin to breathe easily again, and that she would smile and talk to them once more.

Suddenly the lights went off, except in one wing of the house. Usually, the lights did not go off together all over the house. But then the lights went off suddenly a second time, and a blanket of darkness covered the whole of Calcutta. No one realized that the light of life in Mother Teresa, a light that had radiated the warmth of love to everyone she met, and especially to the poorest of the poor, had also gone out.

EPILOGUE: THE FUNERAL

Mother Teresa's life slipped away at 8.30 on the evening of 5 September 1997, but Sister Nirmala did not confirm the sad news until 9.30 p.m. In spite of all the excellent doctors, the correct medicines and the loving care of the sisters, she had finally died as she wished, slipping away quietly in the darkness, just as so many of the people she had tended had done. She went home to Jesus, as she had desired, on a First Friday, in the month of September, when the 100th anniversary of the death of her beloved St Teresa of the Child Jesus was celebrated.

Mother Teresa's body was taken to the chapel and wreathed in flowers, and people came in their hundreds, crowding around in the middle of the night as if it were the middle of the day. At the first Mass offered for Mother Teresa, Father Gray spoke about two women who loved each other very dearly, and who were talking just then in heaven about their children on earth. He was speaking about Mother Teresa and Our Lady.

Messages of condolence came flooding in from all over the world, and the Indian government decided to give Mother

Teresa a state funeral. Her body was embalmed and kept for some time with the sisters and brothers, and when her body was taken from the mother house, the sisters tried to sing through their tears, 'God will take care of you'.

Mother Teresa's body lay in state for a week at St Thomas's, the very church she had entered first on her arrival in India. Flowers arrived in truckloads, so many that they had to be removed to make room for the people who came to see her. There were so many, in fact, that the sisters were able to offer a flower touched to Mother Teresa's body to each person as they left. A never-ending flow of people moved past her body, for days on end.

The whole country was affected by her death. Extra trains had to be laid on. There were even twenty-seven extra flights from Delhi. All the shops sold out of flowers and cards and pictures of Mother Teresa. Around the body, Masses were celebrated continuously by priests and mourners of different parishes and were also celebrated all over the world. Speaking finally at a special Mass for the Missionaries of Charity congregation, Father Joseph said:

Tonight we place at your feet what we have: our misunderstanding, our unforgiveness, our lack of compassion, our lack of love for each other, our jealousy, envy, hurting words, our resentments. Receive it, Mother, from the hearts of your children, with the promise to look forward to a new future, a new society, a new love.

The day of the funeral was a day of national mourning in India, when flags flew at half-mast. The American Senate voted to observe that day as a day of national recognition. The coffin, draped in the national flag of India, was carried by army officers to be placed on the same gun carriage that had borne the bodies of Mahatma Gandhi and Nehru. The Funeral Mass was held in Netajee Stadium, and the police found it difficult to control the crowds who were milling around, breaking the barricades.

The words, 'When I was thirsty, you gave me drink' were written beside the crucifix on the altar, and the words 'To our Mother with love' were inscribed on the candle that burned on the altar. The chief celebrant was His Eminence Cardinal Sodano, representative of the Holy Father himself. There were six cardinals and several archbishops and bishops to concelebrate the Mass. Representatives of the very poorest of the poor, whom Mother Teresa had served all her life, found a place beside the dignitaries at the funeral. Love for a tiny nun had united them all, as the children of the same God the Father.

The Funeral Mass began with the words of the Indian poet Rabindranath Tagore, 'Make our lives holy; touch them with the sparks of fire'. A message from the Holy Father reminded all gathered, irrespective of political affiliation, caste, creed and nationality, that Mother Teresa was an example of firm belief in God, and that she stood steady on the principle that love is what is needed for the poor.

After a three-hour service, the funeral procession took Mother Teresa's body to her last resting place in a special sepulchre that had been prepared for her on the ground floor of the mother house of the congregation. The final ceremonies were private to the congregation themselves, and a salute of rifle fire rang out in the street as her body was lowered into the tomb.

That tomb stands there today and the simple inscription on the white marble is Mother Teresa's message to us, 'As I have loved you, you too love one another'.